Johannes Brahms

CLASSIC *f*M LIFELINES

B JOHANNES RAHMS

AN ESSENTIAL GUIDE TO HIS LIFE AND WORKS

JONATHON BROWN

PAVILION

First published in Great Britain in 1996 by
PAVILION BOOKS LIMITED
26 Upper Ground, London SE1 9PD

Edited and designed by Castle House Press, Llantrisant, South Wales
Cover designed by Bet Ayer

A CIP catalogue record for this book is available
from the British Library

ISBN 1 85793 967 0

Set in Lydian and Caslon
Printed and bound in Great Britain by Mackays of Chatham

2 4 6 8 10 9 7 5 3 1

This book can be ordered direct from the publisher.
Please contact the Marketing Department.
But try your bookshop first.

Contents

ACKNOWLEDGMENTS

A conversation with the violinist Ernst Kovacic in a bar in Glasgow changed my ideas about Brahms and I shall not forget my debt to him also for showing me Vienna and making feel at home when I had none. Thanks, too, to Kirsty; I had nearly forgotten that Mars Bar is a partial anagram of Brahms.

Hospitality and more has come from Don and Pam Stevens, and Cécile Perrin made life easier at the right moment. My sister organized dispatch of material to me from the UK to France, and without Thomas Spronken no blips or beeps could have been transmitted back to the publisher's computer.

Everyone at Castle House Press has put up with me generously and I am grateful for what I shall think of as the pruning, weeding and watering required. Thanks to Riviera Radio in Monte-Carlo, I have been able to share some of my investigation of recordings with listeners, even borrowing some discs from them – most usefully from Lois Clymer.

The book is dedicated to Peggy Donnelly, not least for the most Brahmsian of sparkling elevenses.

A NOTE FROM THE EDITORS

A biography of this type inevitably contains numerous references to pieces of music. The paragraphs are also peppered with 'quotation marks', since much of the tale is told through reported speech.

Because of this, and to make things more accessible for the reader as well as easier on the eye, we decided to simplify the method of typesetting the names of musical works. Conventionally this is determined by the nature of the individual work, following a set of rules whereby some pieces appear in italics, some in italics and quotation marks, others in plain roman type and others still in roman and quotation marks.

In this book, the names of all musical works are simply set in italics. Songs and arias appear in italics and quotation marks.

CHAPTER I

BRAHMS THE CLASSIC?
BRAHMS THE ROMANTIC?
BRAHMS THE WHAT?

Brahms became a popular composer within his own lifetime and his popularity has been expanding ever since. Symphony orchestra records show that Brahms customarily ranks second or third in their performance league tables. The old, catch-phrase question, '*Aimez-vous Brahms?* ', is an entirely rhetorical one – everyone loves Brahms.

In his own lifetime, it was said that there were 'the three B's: Bach, Beethoven and Brahms'. People were anxious to find a successor to Beethoven, who had died in 1827. Born in 1833, Brahms was cursed with the praise that his *First Symphony* was 'Beethoven's Tenth'; 'cursed' because Brahms's *First Symphony* stands perfectly well as Brahms's First on his own terms. Brahms was Brahms, and very good at it too. We love good old Brahms, his voluptuous but strict music, his good-natured bad temper. On the other hand, the great pianist Artur Schnabel warned against *Bier, Bart und Bauch*, that is, Brahms seen in terms of 'the Three B's of beer, beard and belly'. The comedian Victor Borge, fond of making ever more sugary a pastiche of the *Cradle Song*, referred either to 'Joey Brahms', or simply to 'Brahms spelt backwards: *Schmarb*'. Everyone loves Brahms – except when they are a *little* tired of him.

And people do tire of him. Even in his lifetime, it was said that 'he cannot exult'; the fact that he does exult perfectly often merely confirms that he gives off very strongly an impression of never doing so. His textures are seldom light or fluffy, be they in symphony or piano 'miniature'. They should be transparent, but few performers, tackling Brahms with excess familiarity and little curiosity, manage that. He becomes 'heavy'. His range of emotions is a shade limited. Yet Cézanne is not valued the less for having painted so many apples or mountains. Still, Brahms was a man of routine in his life and while routine can give us an idea of productivity, it also suggests at worst sterility or at any rate repetition. Brahms can start to seem limited.

So, paradox and contradiction abound. His music can be ransacked for sentimentality and equally for a contrapuntal vigour unique since J.S. Bach – often enough both in the same piece. For the uncompromisingly theoretical composer Arnold Schoenberg he, of all people, was the great 'revolutionary', yet his work alludes to the baroque more thoroughly than that of any of his contemporaries. Few composers supply us with as robust an erotic relish and yet, to the outside world, he lived a busy, ordered and disciplined bachelor life. By his bed he kept a Bible that he could 'find in the dark', and quote by heart, and he wrote Biblical settings of greater depth and weight than any contemporary – yet his atheism shocked his friends.

This great revolutionary had his favourite tavern in Vienna and disliked having to go to others. It was called 'The Red Hedgehog'; suitably enough, for Brahms was a prickly character accustomed both to tease his friends and to protect his privacy with quips and barbs but who, like Wagner, wrote simply the most powerful music of tender love in the repertoire.

Although we know Brahms's dates, there is also something of a paradox in the way in which he tends to be placed in history. That is to say, the avuncular, almost teddy-bear figure, tends to be happily planted in a corner, out of the stream of history and certainly in the past. The conductor Wilhelm Furtwängler (1886–1954), by far his most insightful and spontaneous interpreter, wrote, in a passage dated 1932 and reprinted in his *Notebooks 1924–1954*:

> *Liszt's works belong to the past, while the effectiveness of Brahms, despite all the efforts to the contrary, continues to grow. . . . Brahms, since his emergence, has been underrated, trivialised, presented as being of no importance, without suffering any damage whatsoever. . . .*
>
> *The living effectiveness of the music of Brahms – in Germany, Scandinavia and the Anglo-Saxon world today one of the most-*

played composers in the concert hall – is suddenly a fact, a reality. And there is nothing I can do about it, these facts interest me more than so many well-meant theories, analyses, attitudes, if the latter do not do justice to the world of facts. And the world of these facts does include the quiet vitality of Brahms's music.

Nonetheless, Brahms's durable popularity seems based on a need audiences have, to escape from historical, perhaps even psychological considerations. Brahms is 'safe'. Schoenberg's essay *Brahms the Revolutionary* is surprising because of its bold sentiment; luckily for safe old Brahms, the gist of it is so technical rather than sentimental that any need to keep Brahms 'safe' can be nourished undeterred.

There are other paradoxes. Brahms felt that some music was too great to be performed and that it should be read in the score instead – for instance Bach's *St Matthew Passion* or Mozart's *Don Giovanni*. On the other hand, in his later years he played his own music with increasingly careless gusto even to the point of acquiring a reputation for playing rather too loud in chamber music. He made one recording, in 1889, on an Edison cylinder, announcing himself across the ferocious crackle as 'Brahms, Johannes Brahms, Dr. Brahms' and storming through the first *Hungarian Dance* like a gipsy horse on the rampage. Yet he made sure that almost all of his orchestral works were made available in his own transcriptions for piano duet so that they could be played by amateurs in the home.

As a revolutionary he kept his innovation within the detail of his own music: he did not like Bruckner's symphonies (too Wagnerian, too indulgent in form), nor Hugo Wolf's songs (undisciplined), nor Richard Strauss's early orchestral pieces, nor Mahler's symphonies, the first two of which he knew – with some horror. He did, however, relax his stubbornness about performance when, having been 'dragged' to hear Mahler conduct *Don Giovanni* in Budapest, he declared that 'to hear the true *Don Giovanni*, you have to go to Budapest.' Mahler was conductor of the opera in Vienna in Brahms's last years and Brahms thought extremely highly of him as a conductor.

Yet the 'safety' of Brahms may prove deceptive. He entwines baroque as well as Romantic temperament to provide a fruitful togetherness. There is purposeful motion, like that of a train, and yet at other times the stillness felt at a pause in a mountain walk. The music achieves a sturdy balance, the solidity of that Brahmsian 'safety' – but safety from what? Brahms is too great an artist not to have defined the danger when he creates the safety.

Danger? In Brahms? In Beethoven we are used to the idea of risk, danger and struggle: we value him for his fist against it all. In Brahms, is not the tendency to imagine that we have, after all, reached a haven after all such upheavals? If so, falsely so.

A quick sign of this is the way in which at the drop of a hat Brahms's music is called 'autumnal'. Ah yes, golden and gorgeous. Yet the divine splendour of autumn is an illusion. Brahms's supposedly golden, autumnal magnificence gives us an apparent even keel, steady, sturdy and safe – but that conceals the choppiest of passages in life. The warm colours of autumn are, after all, the death throes of nature, a *rigor mortis*. It is all an illusion. And Furtwängler was shrewd, in the last year of his own life, to note of Brahms that he was 'the arch-enemy of all false illusions'.

Which illusions? There are two. One is Love, the other God. Brahms believed in love but behaved towards it with fear; he did not believe in God nor any promise of life after death, yet from his godlessness stemmed his absolute belief in human love. In *'Auf dem Kirchhofe'*, Op.105 No.4, a late song telling of the dilapidated state of some tombstones, Brahms revels heavily in the pun between '*Gewesen*' and '*Genesen*', the first being the word to signify 'deceased', the second meaning 'cured'. In his four last songs, the first three are bleak and bitter songs of death with no indication of redemption; the last takes Luther's translation of St Paul's passage declaring that, of Faith, Hope and Love (*Glaube, Hoffnung, Liebe*), the greatest is Love. There is no doubt of the supreme significance of that word for Brahms.

Whatever Schoenberg may have had to say about technique, Brahms was this much a revolutionary too: he is the first great composer to be plainly and without equivocation an atheist. In Beethoven's *Missa Solemnis* (1819/23), in the soprano's final, almost frantic, plea for peace, '*Dona nobis pacem*', it is clear that Beethoven doubts that any God hears the cry. In Wagner's *Parsifal* (1877/82), the symbolism of Gethsemane is stood on its head and we have an anti-Christ who does not have to be sacrificed for the redemption of Man. Equivocation persists if only because of the imagery Wagner uses to stand the Christian myth on its head. In Brahms's last songs, which he entitled *Four Serious Songs*, he strides off stage with a clear juxtaposition of two sentiments – that Death is final, and that the greatest power in life is Love.

In Brahms the momentum of 'avoidance' is an underrated but a major force. It can take the shape of bluster, or sometimes a sort of recollection in tranquility. The tranquility, the balance, are both edgy. Often he uses oscillating themes that rock on arpeggios, and we can watch chords split open into lines of melody – a process that expresses a human vacillation and blinking doubt or disbelief that we all recognize, yet a process that also suggests Brahms at the keyboard, the weight of his hands using the thumb as a pivot on which to rock, a central pivot that brings well-earned stability to our troubles. The evident humanity of Brahms's music owes much to the way it expresses both his gait and his grasp, his career and his caress.

Brahms's huge strength is that he understands doubt or disbelief from within and takes us by the collar, refusing to let us avoid things, refusing to let doubt have the better of us, and leading us to a culminating, sometimes even ecstatic sense of well-being despite all disbelief. It is an odd reflection on our culture that we have come to assume there may be more to learn, on joy and regret, on power and fear, and on the repression and expression of sexual energy, from the pseudo-science of Freud or the old-hatted flannel of the New Age than from one such as Brahms. If Brahms has remained important today, it is for the human insights he serves up with such terrifying, enervating honesty.

CHAPTER 2
THE EARLY YEARS
(1833–53)

- ♦ *Musical background and early promise*
- ♦ *First piano lessons and performances*
- ♦ *First compositions*
- ♦ *Meets violinists Reményi and Joachim*
- ♦ *Introduction to Liszt's circle*
- ♦ *Presents himself to Schumann*

Johannes Brahms was born, in Hamburg, in the *Gangeviertel*, a seedy area by the docks, on 7 May 1833. It was a poor area, but that did nothing to diminish the sense of pride that the inhabitants took in their city, at that time an independent port squeezed between Schleswig-Holstein to the north and the rest of the myriad German states to the south. The neighbourhood's name indicates that it was a *quarter* riddled with *lanes* and narrow streets; there were canals too and the whole place was a red-light district.

His family was deep-rooted in Northern Germany. The name is an old one, though it was given as Brahmst on a certificate held by Brahms's father. The composer's great-grandfather had been a cabinet-maker or at any rate a carpenter, who lived in Brunsbüttel, on the mouth of the Elbe within fifty miles of Hamburg, and his grandfather had been an innkeeper at Heide, a dozen miles due north of there.

Brahms's father, Johann Jakob, was born in 1806. He was the first musician in the family and had achieved his modest career after a struggle with his own father's disapproval of the trade. According to Brahms in later years, his father had twice run away from home to pursue his vocation. A musician of robust confidence in his limited but adequate ability, he acted mainly as double-bass player but also occasionally as horn player in the local band, and even bugler in the Hamburg civic guard. He was certainly a lively character and would fit all our fondest preconceptions of a jovial, tuneful good sort at the taverns and bandstands.

Jakob had gone to Hamburg to seek work and there had married Johanna Henrika Christiane Nissen in 1830; it was an advantageous match, given his scraping circumstances. Born in 1789, and of slenderly aristocratic descent, she was of a higher social station than he and more practical in everyday matters. Their first child, Elisabeth Wilhelmine Louise, known usually as Elise, was born in 1831, Johannes next and after him, in 1835, Friedrich Fritz. The younger brother was forever cursed in later life in Hamburg with the nickname 'the wrong Brahms', a situation not helped by Brahms's practical joke, in the days when his beard was unfamiliar to the public, of sending autograph-hunters and admirers off to chase Fritz instead.

THE YOUNG PUPIL

Brahms's ordinary education began in what his usually most flowery and digressively charming biographer Walter Niemann refers to bluntly as a 'bad private school'. In later life he made up for his haphazard schooling, collecting and reading books with a passion. In his childhood, however, the emphasis was quickly to fall upon his musical gifts and his musical education began when he was five or six. His father was determined to see his son achieve the same career and satisfaction from music as he had himself and had the same ambitions for Fritz as well. It was at this time, in 1840, that the death of the Alsterpavillon sextet's double-bass player gave Jakob his proud promotion from deputy horn to become the spa band's permanent bass player.

Very soon Brahms had shown an uncanny, natural musical sense and an ambition, distressing enough to a seasoned band player like his father, to play the piano. It was bad enough that Brahms was already keen to compose, there being, his father was sure, no money in composition except possibly in band arrangements; but the piano, of all instruments! His father relented nonetheless, perhaps because at least with the piano his son could make some money in bars – such work might earn the traditional fee of 'two thalers and all you can drink!'

Brahms took his first piano lessons in 1840, from one Otto Cossel, admired as a teacher but luckily also sufficiently down at heel to accept the little that Jakob could afford. Brahms quickly displayed the skills and ease of a true prodigy. Subsequent efforts by wistful biographers to deny that in these years he played the piano in brothels as well as in the ordinary taverns (a fine distinction in any case, in the dockside lanes of Hamburg) reek more of preconceived horror than researched fact. At any rate, the youngster Brahms was soon in demand, requested also to play at the smarter taverns. By the age of fifteen, besides his extraordinary proficiency on piano, Brahms was already able to deputize for his father on violin or cello, even on horn if need be. Something of a career seemed to beckon. Those three other instruments remained his favourites throughout his life, until a late flourishing of interest in the clarinet.

Cossel's influence should not be washed away in history. Brahms was certainly never a man to deny or conceal or stint praise and gratitude where he felt they might be due; in Cossel's slightly unfashionable choice of classic repertoire as well as his style of teaching, Brahms was moulded in a way that he never regretted. Though he worked hard at all stages in his career, Brahms always had an instinctively sure touch and his early training happily suited his natural gifts. Cossel was an excellent teacher, his excellence doubtless further fired by this exceptional pupil, yet eventually he gave away his greatest pupil in an act of rare wisdom and generosity.

The situation was this: an impresario passing through Hamburg invited young Brahms to make a tour of the United States as a child prodigy. Brahms was, of course, greatly tempted by the project; his father even more so. It is easy to look down at the show-biz razzamatazz with disdain and dismay but Brahms's parents were sufficiently flattered – and in need – that not only did they endorse the scheme but even went so far as to sell his mother's small shop in readiness for the trip. In his wisdom Cossel was set against the frightful scheme. However, he could only prevail against Jakob's natural inclination towards fame and fortune by transferring Brahms to the care of Eduard Marxsen (1806–87), Cossel's own teacher and by far the most distinguished of Hamburg's piano teachers. Marxsen was a serious man; he would not approve of this offer, Cossel reckoned. Nor did he, not at all. The device worked. Jakob's enthusiasm was calmed, Brahms was spared the trip and Marxsen gained for himself the pupil that outshone all others – but to Cossel's selfless cost. And at none to Jakob: Marxsen did not charge for the lessons.

Brahms was lucky, too, in his second teacher. Marxsen was an interesting musician of the highest standing in Hamburg. Among his compositions was a quantity of work for piano left hand and Brahms played one such piece at one of his very first concerts organized by his teacher. (Brahms later wrote an arrangement for piano left hand of the *Chaconne* from Bach's *Partita in D minor*, for solo violin.) What is more, it was Brahms, behind the scenes, who later encouraged the publisher Simrock to issue a piano method of Marxsen's, a didactic extravaganza entitled *One Hundred Variations on a Folksong*.

Cossel's teaching, insofar as we can tell, had been inspirational, even though he lamented Brahms's 'distracted' energies spent on composition (of all things!) and had quite strict ideas about his training. By contrast Marxsen, who had originally been marked out for the ministry, had a method that was decidedly authoritarian as well as disciplinarian.

This sense of discipline and detail became a hallmark of Brahms's working life. Time and again Brahms reveals himself to be fastidious in his creativity and intricate in his technique while the music that results sounds astonishingly improvizational and unfettered in passion, swing and sweep. His taste for counterpoint and intricacy both of texture and rhythm also showed itself from the start. On the other hand, the fastidious quality can sometimes seem to be a limitation, in the reluctance with which Brahms issued finished work and in the relatively circumscribed range of emotions that he expressed.

Yet the fastidiousness has another side, most movingly present in the works of his last six years, in the 1890s, and that is a sort of curiosity, not to say fascination, with the very fabric and stuff of music. It is as if he is looking in on the mechanism of sound, dwelling on the smallest morsel as the germ of an entire piece. Such fascination had also shown itself from the start, albeit gingerly enough: Marxsen told of how, given a sonata by Weber to prepare, Brahms returned the following week wishing to play it in two quite separate manners, bringing out entirely different aspects of the music.

At any rate, with insightful cunning, Marxsen contained Brahms's talent for improvization and composition. He did not immediately encourage him to compose. Instead he allowed technique and discipline at the keyboard to infiltrate his musicianship as composer. Brahms was made to study Bach and Beethoven especially and was thus brought up to write music 'from the inside', so to speak. The fashionable, dazzling virtuoso vehicles of his day are quintessentially decorative music, written from the outside, for effect. In those days, a grounding in the 'classics' such as Bach, Beethoven and to a lesser extent Clementi, Hummel or Weber, was by no means the obvious choice. With this method Marxsen nurtured both the pianist and the composer.

It suited Brahms well. He flourished. As his compositional skills became evident, Marxsen was also impressed by what he nicely referred to later as 'a rare acuteness of mind that enchanted me'.

His character as pianist and composer developed hand in hand with his character as a young man. Throughout his life, Brahms had a modest, homely, simple and genuine sense of worth. This clearly stemmed from the warmth not only of his home life but also of his relationships with his two teachers. No matter how renowned Brahms was to become, he did not lose these values – nor his gratitude to his teachers. His jovial relationship with his father, too, many years later, after the death of his mother, delighted his Viennese friends who met them having a grand time together. With friends he was, as far as tact went, notoriously accident-prone but his sense of mischief and indeed his capacity to hurt people's feelings belong to the character of a man blinded a little by his own infectious enthusiasm for life.

Brahms treasured companionship, the sense of togetherness in an enterprise, whether tackling new music with his teacher or setting off on a bracing walk with friends. In academic discussion of his orchestration, for example, much can be made of the musicological meaning and effect of Brahms's taste for the already old-fashioned but less flexible horn without valves; yet just as attractive as any theory is the idea that that was simply the kind of dented old horn Brahms was brought up with in his home and in the parks. As with many 'revolutionaries', in many other things he resisted change.

True, he became a rich man and was capable of a gruff

behaviour that might have been mistaken for arrogance, yet neither his money nor his self-esteem led him astray. On the contrary, he could look back on his rise from these humblest of beginnings with wry humour. He was never slow to help anyone, often anonymously, when he could, Dvořák benefiting from this most notably. When the latter was in his mid-fifties and Brahms wanted to persuade him to move to Vienna, in 1896, Brahms said to him with characteristic common sense and a thump of the table, 'Look here, Dvořák, you have a lot of children to support, I have practically nobody. If you need anything, my fortune is at your disposal.'

THE YOUNG PERFORMER

Brahms made his first public appearance at the age of ten, playing at a concert given to raise money for his own education. Thanks to participation by his father's cronies, the concert included Beethoven's *Wind Quintet* and one of Mozart's piano quartets, as well as a study by one Henri Herz that Brahms himself played. His first public concert as such took place four years later, on 20 November 1847, in Hamburg; he played Thalberg's *Fantasia on Themes from Bellini's 'Norma'*.

This alone gives the flavour of the start to his musical career. In form loosely construed as variations mish-mashed usually from a popular opera, such pieces flourished in the exuberance of the then new, flashy piano virtuosity associated most of all with Liszt. Sometimes music of this sort is called *pluies de perles*, a 'shower of pearls', to describe the cascades of notes in the treble that decorate or disguise the tune. It was all the rage. Franz Liszt (1811–86) was then at the height of his fame and his rivals at the height of their clamour for his throne. It gives an idea of the gladiatorial frenzy of such music-making that in 1837, Sigismond Thalberg (1812–71) and Liszt had staged a 'duel' in the Paris home of the Princess Cristina Belgiojoso-Trivulzio, of which the 'play-off' involved exactly such cascading and frothily embellished permutations and contortions of the season's most-hummed tunes: Thalberg on themes from Rossini's *Moses*, Liszt from Pacini's *La Niobe*.

A circus mood persists even today, on the concert platform and in the output of the big record companies anxious to unveil astonishing new pianistic wizardry before us as regularly as possible. All the same, there is a slight whiff of the museum about it: today's pianists seldom go so far as to compose their own display pieces, nor even cadenzas to concertos – exceptions in the stereo age include Leonard Pennario, Georges Cziffra and Friedrich Gulda. Brahms on the other hand was born into an era in which this gladiatorial element was vividly and wholeheartedly alive. He did not avoid the fray for which his virtuosity well equipped him. He could only overcome the shallow vulgarity of it all by tackling it front-on and in his youth he did exactly that – yet he kept his other eye on higher things.

It is an early example of the sense of balance deep within Brahms's character. Normally a shy young man, he also displayed the bouts of defensive exhibitionist energy that can go with such reserve. His earliest piano compositions make for a perfect example of this. They were written during his twenties and include no less than six extended sets of virtuoso variations, after which he never returned to that form; indeed, for over a dozen years thereafter he did not write music for solo piano at all. He had had enough. For all that, these variations were not written on popularly-hummed operatic themes in the showy manner of Thalberg and his sort, they were to serious themes by Schumann and Handel and to one of his own, the nearest to the 'vulgar' being the set based on a Hungarian dance and two sets to an evergreen theme from a *Caprice* for solo violin by Paganini.

Brahms's first full solo concert, which followed in September 1848, again in Hamburg, included a *Fantasia on Themes from Rossini's 'William Tell'* by Theodor Döhler (1814–56; despite his name he was actually an Italian whose greatest fame may simply be that Brahms played him on this occasion). The only piece of music in any way serious was a fugue by Bach – serious enough. He played a *Serenade for left hand* by Marxsen but still no composition of his own. Until a more successfully publicized event the following spring, that is, at which he played two such flashy efforts, one by Thalberg (on themes from Mozart's *Don Giovanni*) and one that he had written himself, a *Fantasia on a Favourite Waltz* that has not survived. The serious work on this occasion? – Beethoven's '*Waldstein*' *Sonata*, Op.53, no less.

He did publish one such display piece: *Souvenir de la Russie*, in the form of *Fantasias on Russian and Bohemian Airs*, written before 1852. It was issued under the pseudonym G.W. Marks, carefully hiding Brahms's identity and mischievously playing upon his teacher's name. The title, *Souvenir*, as with *Reminiscences*, was a popular term for florid variations and fantasies of a more or less exotic sort and did not imply that the composer had set foot anywhere in sight of the place of which the piece is supposedly a recollection. Brahms had never been outside Germany, let alone travelled to Russia. But he would have heard an international mixture of popular music in the dockside areas of Hamburg and his ear was exceptional.

There was another side to the music Brahms encountered in Hamburg – that was the serious, the classical. A singular event in the calendar of 1848 epitomized this serious aspect and was to be a landmark in the composer's life: a performance of Beethoven's *Violin Concerto*, with Joseph Joachim the soloist.

TWO VIOLINISTS: REMÉNYI AND JOACHIM

Brahms's early life had centred around the piano, yet the decisive encounters of his life that were now to take place, in his late teens, were with two violinists. The first of these was Eduard Reményi (1828–98), three years Brahms's senior, and a wandering, wild, possibly roguish character of Jewish-Hungarian blood.

The meeting with Reményi may have been as early as 1849 or 1850, when the violinist found himself in Hamburg, in flight from the Hungarian revolution. At any rate it was not until 1852/53 that he and Brahms agreed to pool their diverse talents as performers. Except for his virtuosic bravado, Reményi seems to have been an entirely different character to Brahms: Reményi's life was spent zig-zagging across the world, taking in appointments to Queen Victoria, a trip to the Far East as part of a world tour, and a flourishsome death, on stage, in California, in 1898, only months after Brahms had died, rather more gently, in bed in Vienna. He wrote transcriptions and a concerto still seemingly unrecorded.

In April 1853 the two young men set off from Hamburg – strolling on foot much of the way – to tour neighbouring villages and towns. It was during this trip that Brahms amazed an audience with a 'trick' that fluent pianists find not too difficult but which invariably leaves the public speechless: finding the piano a semitone out of tune, he transposed his accompaniment accordingly as he played. Brahms also had the knack of not taking the music with him on such trips: he knew it all by heart.

And most important of all, it was during this trip, at Hanover, that Reményi introduced Brahms to a former schoolfellow. That person was none other than Joseph Joachim (1831–1907). Only a couple of years older than Brahms, Joachim was already a celebrity as a player; he was also *Konzertmeister*, or leader of the orchestra, as well as Music Master, at the court of the King of Hanover. His first public appearance, at the age of seven, had been a concert with Mendelssohn accompanying. At thirteen he had made a first tour of England, a country with which he would have close ties throughout his life, and he went on to champion Brahms's music there.

Today, Joachim's most frequently-played works are his cadenzas to the concertos by Beethoven and Brahms. His own compositions – apart from violin pieces there are overtures and songs – are neglected even in our present era of musical archaeology, yet his instinct and inspiration were not at all negligible. Like Brahms but unusually for the time, he wrote no opera. The great musicologist, pianist and conductor Sir Donald Francis Tovey, who knew Joachim in his last years, was a champion of the so-called '*Hungarian' Violin Concerto*, of which Brahms himself wrote that it was full of 'restrained beauty and so calm, so deep and warm in feeling that it is a joy.'

Like Reményi, Joachim was of Hungarian descent but unlike him he had a deeply proper streak to his nature. He may have been a shade embarrassed to receive this dusty pair of itinerant contemporaries, Reményi especially representing to him the vulgar side of their profession as violinists. On hearing Brahms play his own compositions, however, Joachim's forgiveness was immediate. A deep bond of admiration and affection was quickly established.

If Reményi had hoped that the glory Brahms attracted everywhere, annoying enough as that was, would reflect upon him, his designs were thwarted – in fact the opposite was true. Joachim, on the other hand, showed an attitude utterly devoid of jealousy or scheme, presenting Brahms as soon as possible to the King, to Liszt and subsequently to the Schumann household, Robert and Clara. Indeed, even when Joachim and Brahms fell out slightly, later on in the long friendship, and relations resumed at a cooler degree, Joachim never allowed that sentiment to detract from his devotion to performance of Brahms's music.

From the outset the two men wrote frequently to each other and two volumes of correspondence survive. At first, Joachim, in mock serious vein, would sign his letters Josephus Joachimus, and these early letters bubble with a youthful sense of musical adventure. There is a typical letter from Brahms to Joachim, written in February 1856 when the two were encouraging each other in counterpoint:

> And then I want to remind you of what you have so often discussed and beg you to let us carry it out, namely, to send one another exercises in counterpoint . . . until we have both become really clever. . . . Why should not two sensible, earnest people like ourselves be able to teach one another far better than any professor could? But do not reply in words – send me your first study in a fortnight.

Brahms also wrote of him at that time:

> Today I bought a small pipe which J. and I smoked during the evening. It made us both very ill, J. especially. I have been admiring J. extremely in his practising of the [Beethoven's] Ninth. If only he were not often too profound for the musicians. But the ladies cannot of course help being delighted, and they are! There is more in J. than in all the young composers put together, how much more. I cannot help thinking about what will become of it. What sort of influence will life have on J.?

Brahms's uncanny human wisdom was in place early in life.

The two violinists appealed to the two sides of Brahms's temperament, the Romantic and the Classical, while also infusing him with a taste for gipsy and Hungarian inflection – normal enough had he been in Vienna but exotic or even vulgar in the north. All these elements come together particularly in his *Piano Sonata No.2*, in which almost unpianistic material is justified on the keyboard by its vivid portrayal of gipsy fiddle-sawing energy.

In the company of one or other of these violinists Brahms found himself on the whirligig of celebrity; Joachim could handle this, but before long Reményi had had enough. They had travelled to Weimar to see Liszt, a journey momentarily delayed by typical problems concerning Reményi and the police. To be greeted by Liszt was an awesome occasion. The Liszt residence at the Villa Altenberg was something of a pretentious environment – a cross between hippy and Bloomsbury. The conversation was mostly carried on in French. It all dismayed young Brahms by its superficiality and falseness; Reményi on the other hand adored the tacky and scheming showmanship of the place.

BRAHMS AND LISZT

Brahms was far too bashful to play before the straggle-haired genius. Liszt solved the problem and took Brahms's manuscript pages from him and played his *Scherzo in E flat minor* at sight, twice, or so the story goes, thereupon requisitioning Brahms for his band of revolutionary followers. (This *Scherzo* was later published as Op.4.)

Brahms admired Liszt as pianist more than as composer however, and could not hide his reservations about the whole place. There later arose a much-told but nonetheless improbable story of his falling asleep while Liszt played his one-movement *Piano Sonata in B minor*. Perhaps this story was a subsequent and vengeful invention on the part of Reményi; if true, the story is surely more a tribute to Liszt's cellar at the Villa Altenberg than a criticism of his rendition of his own masterpiece. Even allowing for their different temperaments, Brahms was not as impressed by the great work as we might expect anyone to be, not only on first hearing it – still today one of the great moments in any musician's early life – but, after all, played by Liszt himself! Perhaps Brahms found it more rambling than compressed, perhaps he found that there was too much flowery writing, perhaps he found the final fugue technically not up to scratch as counterpoint. So, perhaps he did doze off after all!

Be that as it may, Brahms was at first welcomed into the Lisztian entourage. There he met composers such as Peter Cornelius (1824–74) and Joseph Joachim Raff (1822–82), no doubt with the hesitant, diffident enthusiasm of one whose genius will far outshine his then more illustrious inferiors. Raff's talent was partly as a clever rather than fluent contrapuntist and his music was mainly symphonic; he wrote eleven symphonies, many with subtitles or programmes, as well as the usual trunk-load of other Romantic pieces, piano transcriptions and so on.

Cornelius, on the other hand, was a lyrical composer (his operas have not entirely disappeared – *The Barber of Bagdad* least of all – and some of his songs rightly remain in the repertoire); in his career appointments he rather followed Wagner about, becoming in the last decade of his life a teacher to Ludwig II of Bavaria. These were perhaps the two most distinguished and the most congenial men Brahms met in Liszt's circle.

It is at this moment and in the almost menacing shadow of Liszt that intrigue and faction begin to spoil the happy story so far. At no time in these early rounds of illustrious introductions and potentially influential social encounters did Brahms show any sign of pressing himself or seeking favour; quite the opposite. Nor, in later life, with the roles reversed, did he care for people seeking such advancement through himself. Liszt's following was indeed a band of hangers-on, but Brahms valued friendship above everything. He felt ill at ease in Liszt's entourage. The usually dim-witted drooling was made worse by the fact that there was something of an official Romantic 'manifesto' for new music underlying it all: the so-called 'New German Music'.

This 'New German Music' was sometimes also called *Zukunfts-musik*, the 'Music of the Future', especially in the case of Liszt's alliance with Wagner. Oddly enough, many of these 'New German' theories were cobbled together by Liszt's band of Poles, Hungarians and others, all taking their lead from the Frenchman Hector Berlioz. The air of partisan loyalties in so fortunate a vocation as music was distressing to the straightforward north German son of a double-bass player. Wide-boy Reményi, on the other hand, found it all extremely attractive and took part with relish – Liszt was always to be grateful to him at the very least, for expanding his understanding of how to handle gipsy music. With enthusiasm, Reményi declared himself a member of the movement.

Brahms did not. He followed Joachim, equally ill-at-ease, to Göttingen, where they gave a concert together. Brahms was a shade disorientated by all he had seen and heard. Later that year he went on a walking holiday by the Rhine, and the trip refreshed Brahms's hold on the new momentum of his career. By the end of it, in September, he had summoned enough courage to present himself to Schumann, in Düsseldorf. Joachim had long wanted to bring the two together and Schumann was to that extent prepared.

Armed with a letter of introduction from Joachim – a strange sort of effective 'passport' that he always had about him – Brahms went literally to Schumann's home and knocked at the door. Schumann gladly let him in.

BRAHMS MEETS SCHUMANN

Robert Schumann (1810–56) was a composer whose genius as well as life-style was altogether more in tune with Brahms's than with the grandiose follies of Liszt's self-styled regal court. Schumann was not a flaunting, would-be king basking in adulation but a domestic man, committed to chamber music and chamber music-making, as was his wife Clara, herself a composer and formidable pianist. Brahms may have expected to stay the afternoon but he was asked to live with the Schumanns and he did so for some weeks. As he first touched the piano keys, Schumann called Clara through to hear; she was never out of Brahms's life from that moment until her death, a year before his. Clara was nine years younger than Schumann, fourteen years older than Brahms.

In the Schumann home he worked away on compositions that only just survived the flames of his own critical censorship, for he had already acquired the habit of burning sketches and scores he did not think up to scratch. One such was the *Hymn to the Veneration of the great Joachim*, a bizarre concoction comprising waltzes for two violins and bass or cello that was only published in 1976. He worked a great deal and studied with Schumann as well as playing duets and trios.

A flavour of the energetic and creative mood of the household during Brahms's stay can be guessed at from the way that, on hearing of the imminent arrival of Joachim himself, Schumann, Brahms and a fellow composer friend called Albert Dietrich conspired between them to write a violin sonata to welcome him. Dietrich wrote the opening movement and Schumann an intermezzo and final movement while Brahms wrote the scherzo, which was only published, with Joachim's sanction, over fifty years later. Joachim had adopted as his personal motto the melancholy but proud tag *Frei aber einsam* ('free but solitary'), and the sonata came to be known as the '*F.A.E. Sonata*'.

One thing missing in Liszt's circle – and this was important to Brahms – was a devotion to the German language and in particular to its poetry. The Schumanns had a passion for the fanciful and Romantic literature of the time, which Brahms was hungry to share. Along with music, the German language provided the unity of culture that was in many respects the guiding model for the political unity they all also sought. The two composers had a particular ear for poetry and there was no greater song-writer alive than Schumann. Brahms's early opus numbers include a dozen songs.

There was also a love of word-play among these friends. Musicians liked mottoes whose initial letters could generate thematic material: Schumann and his circle loved such 'secret' devices – his motto for Clara was concealed in music written while her father disapproved of their romance, and to the same purpose he had used material from Beethoven's song-cycle '*To the distant beloved*' in the *Fantasy in C major*, Op.17. In deference but also in gently pointed defiance, Brahms was associated with an altered version of Joachim's, *Frei aber froh* ('free but cheery'), and in 1859 he imposed a motto on the choir that he conducted: *Fix oder Nix*, 'on the dot or not at all'. The note pattern F–A–F appears with hearty regularity throughout Brahms's themes, though it is unlikely that he actually invented it. It is at any rate specially conspicuous in the *Third Symphony*, while in the final movement of his *First* he had used Joachim's motto F–A–E. It may be of significance that of words whose sound is related to these initials, Joachim's F–A–E resembles most of all *fähig*, a word meaning able or capable, while Brahms's F–A–F resembles *Pfaff*, a parson or cleric!

Schumann, meantime, was working on an article for the *Neue Zeitschrift für Musik*, the journal of musical opinion that he had founded twenty years before but for which he had written nothing in a decade. Its editorial policy had drifted away from his own views. Signed merely 'R.S.' and entitled *Neue Bahnen*, this was an article heralding the arrival in the musical world of a man who would forge such 'New Paths' – Johannes Brahms. Given the way the others styled themselves as the 'New German' school, this was a carefully provocative title. Schumann had founded the paper not least to keep the public eye peeled for new or rising talent, and the expression with which he exclaimed his own 'spotting' of Chopin – on the basis merely of his early *Variations on 'Là ci darem la mano' from Mozart's 'Don Giovanni'* – became his most lasting monument as a commentator: 'Hats off, gentlemen, a genius!' He wished to say the same now of his new friend.

The article on Brahms was published in the edition of 28 October 1853. Schumann's florid style does not conform to today's preference for drearily risk-free or abstrusely technical circumspection, nor was his selection of the other talents that had emerged in those years the selection we would make today. Despite all of this, however, its quick recognition of Brahms was exact and effective. It is a typical touch that Schumann had the courtesy to send a copy of the issue to Brahms's parents. He also sent a small portrait of himself to Brahms, who thanked him in a letter ending, 'You have rejoiced the hearts of two or three worthy people by your attention and I am for life, Yours, Brahms.'

Omitting a little of the preamble, this is what Schumann wrote:

> I thought that . . . there must and would suddenly appear one whose destiny should be to express the spirit of our age in the highest and most ideal fashion, one who should not reveal his mastery by a gradual development, but spring, like Minerva, fully armed from the head of Jove. And now he has come, a young creature over whose cradle the Graces and heroes have kept watch. His name is Johannes Brahms; he comes from Hamburg, where he has worked in quiet obscurity, though trained in the most difficult rules of his art by the enthusiastic solicitude of an admirable master . . . and recently introduced to me by a revered and well-known artist.
>
> Even in his outward appearance he bore all the distinguishing signs which proclaim him one of the elect. Sitting down to the piano, he began to open up regions of wonder. We were drawn more and more into charmed circles. Add to this a technique of absolute genius, which turned the piano into an orchestra of wailing or exultant voices. There were sonatas – which were rather veiled symphonies – songs whose poetry one could have understood even without knowing the words, though a deep singing melody runs throughout them – some detached piano pieces, some of a demonic nature, though most graceful in form – then sonatas for violin and piano – quartets for stringed instruments – and all so different from one another that each seemed to spring from a different source. And then it seemed as though, rushing onward like a river, he combined them all as though in a waterfall, with

the rainbow of peace playing on its downward streaming waters, while butterflies flutter round it on the banks, accompanied by the song of nightingales.

If only he would point his magic wand to where the might of mass, in chorus and orchestra, lends him its power, yet more wondrous glimpses into the mysteries of the spirit world await us. May the highest genius give him strength for this! And indeed there is every prospect of it, since another genius, that of modesty, also dwells within him. His comrades hail him on his first journey out into the world, where wounds perhaps await him, but laurels and palms besides. We welcome him as a stout fighter.

CHAPTER 3
AWAY FROM LISZT, TOWARDS SCHUMANN
(the mid-1850s)

- ♦ First publication of his compositions
- ♦ Leipzig, Liszt and Berlioz
- ♦ Schumann's madness
- ♦ Brahms's passion for Clara Schumann
- ♦ Schumann's death
- ♦ Court appointment at Detmold

Schumann's article had one immediate effect – publishers were now seeking to put Brahms's work into print. He wrote to Joachim that 'Dr. Schumann' was putting his music to the publishers 'with such earnestness and determination that I feel quite bewildered.' The publication of music was a major source of income for any composer, increasingly so as urban Europe became well populated with competent amateur musicians – and pianos.

The choice of pieces to publish was one that exercised Brahms a good deal and it was already clear that whatever he did not publish he would destroy. This was to be his method through-out his life. As one who had quickly found himself in the midst of the bickering and envy-ridden factions of contemporary music at the highest level, he could not afford to issue anything that was not what he then thought was his absolute best. *'Fix oder Nix'*, after all. The manuscript of the *Piano Sonata* Op.1 is marked *'Piano Sonata No.4 '*, which means that, in addition to the *Piano Sonata* Op.2, which we know was written earlier than Op.1, there were therefore at least two others that Brahms at first counted but then suppressed. The three sonatas that eventually saw the light of day are sizeable works; if the two he destroyed were on anything like the same scale, this is no less than an hour's music.

He gave a good deal of thought even to the order of publication of these pieces and consulted his new band of supporting friends, including Joachim, who wrote with flamboyant wisdom: 'It really seems to me immaterial (from a higher standpoint and therefore from yours) with which of your works you first declaim to the world: "*I am!*" ' A heavenly vision remains a heavenly vision even if it begins by merely showing the world . . . its big toe.' Schumann had suggested an order that lacked punch, arranging the pieces that way, he said, 'for the sake of variety'; Joachim's order was bolder, more robustly street-wise, with the standard-bearing Opus 1 marked down as containing no less than both the big first piano sonatas that were subsequently issued in a more manageable form, separately, as Opp.1 and 2.

In the end, the publishing house of Breitkopf & Härtel took the two piano sonatas, a set of six songs and the *Scherzo* (actually the earliest of all his pieces, written in 1850/52), giving them respectively the opus numbers 1 to 4; the house of Senff took the third sonata and another set of six songs, with opus numbers 5 and 6. They were unable to take a violin sonata – it did not fit their 'house style' – and the piece was eventually lost.

Thus Brahms launched himself on the music scene in no uncertain manner. To appear with three big sonatas marked him as a serious composer in the tradition established by Beethoven; to add in the songs balanced that with intimacy and homeliness, in the tradition upheld by Schumann. The importance of sonata form at the time has been neatly summarized by the scholar and pianist Charles Rosen: 'After Beethoven, the sonata was the vehicle of the sublime. The proof of craftsmanship was the fugue, but the proof of greatness was the sonata. Only through the sonata, it seemed, could the highest musical ambitions be realized. The opera, because of its extramusical aspects, was only a second best. Pure music in its highest state was sonata.'

This 'sublime' challenge led composers on to all sorts of absurdities and botch-shots. Among the most absurd were attempts to orchestrate Beethoven's grand and difficult '*Hammerklavier*' *Sonata*; Brahms's teacher Marxsen orchestrated Beethoven's *Violin Sonata in A* (the '*Kreutzer*'), Op.47 (1802), and Brahms himself conducted Joachim's orchestration of the *Grand Duo in C*, D.812

(1824) by Schubert, originally written for piano duet. As for botch-shots, Rosen gives as an example a final movement of a piano sonata by Hummel in which the composer – himself one of Beethoven's teachers! – strives to work his material around quotation from Mozart's suitably sublime '*Jupiter*' *Symphony*, a moment of which Rosen says drily, 'It is less clear whether he is varying it on purpose or whether he doesn't remember exactly how it goes.'

'Spotting influences' in new pieces was a favourite form of critical game-playing in those days (it still is) and the wiseacres moved in immediately, pointing to the stamp of Beethoven's '*Hammerklavier*' *Sonata* in the *Sonata No.1* and traces of Chopin in the *Scherzo*, if only in its title and proportions. Brahms's response to any such criticism became famous: 'Any ass can see that.'

It is difficult to imagine how any serious composer could avoid being in awe of the '*Hammerklavier*', a vast stretch of extraordinary piano music on an unprecedented scale, written in 1818/19. Certainly the first two of Schubert's last three sonatas were conceived in that shadow and tackle similarly energetic material – the *Piano Sonata in C minor*, D.958, and the *Piano Sonata in A*, D.959, both written immediately after Beethoven's death, in 1828. But the Schubert pieces were twenty-five and thirty years old when Brahms issued his sonata; the more recent influence of Schumann had been just as decisive upon Brahms, giving him many clues on the handling of transitional passages and on rhythmic progression. Brahms may or may not have played the piece in public, but he most certainly knew well Schumann's tribute to Beethoven, the great *Fantasy in C*, Op.17, written in 1836 and dedicated to Liszt.

There was, from the start, an angular or even jagged kind of music coming from Brahms, in the sonatas especially – he was establishing a reputation now for his own rough-edged character. Indeed, of all the earlier writers, Brahms's angular music most seems to resemble the sometimes erratic or eccentric piano writing of Clementi, which Brahms would have known better than we do today. Muzio Clementi (1752–1832) was one of the first composers to use the tricky key of F sharp minor for a sonata, and Schumann's extended and expansive *Sonata No.1*, Op.11 (1835), is in the same key. Both works influenced Brahms just as much as Beethoven – the slow movement of the Clementi uncannily like Brahms's slow movement in his Op.1. The influence of Clementi lasted well into Brahms's work too, helping to shape the rhythmic patterns of the last movement of the *Symphony No.2*.

Whatever the influences, Brahms's characteristics were in evidence right away. The music had a marvellously enthusiastic vigour, either emphatic, like a fist on the table, or improvizational, like the foot-stamping of a fiddler. It was never bombastic or empty and was always balanced by exceptionally tender writing. He had made his mark.

LEIPZIG

During 1853, Brahms spent some time in Leipzig, an important musical centre still associated most of all with Mendelssohn (who had died in 1847), but also the location of the head office of his publishers. Here, Brahms again encountered the partisan musical world he so disliked; in particular, the unquestioning reverence for Mendelssohn made Leipzig a city not always to his taste. It was a city slow to cherish Brahms in return, and in his later life a triumph in Leipzig became a special event against the odds.

Liszt was in Leipzig at the time, to hear Berlioz conduct. Berlioz, who had then just turned fifty, was at the height of his fame. Liszt himself was on the point of finishing his masterpiece, the *Piano Sonata in B minor*, a massive piece in one movement, culminating in a fugue. (In exchange for the dedication of the *Fantasy*, Liszt dedicated his sonata to Schumann.) Through him Brahms renewed contact with Reményi. There was a mood of excitement about the place that Brahms both relished and resisted. Berlioz praised young Brahms but the latter could see that others praised him emptily only in order to fall in with the exotic, wandering Frenchman. It all simply reminded him of the fawning cliquishness he had wished to avoid. Nonetheless, late in 1853 Brahms gave his first concert in Leipzig, attended by both Liszt and Berlioz. He played his *Sonata*, Op.1.

In Leipzig he also met such musicians as the pioneering piano virtuoso Ignaz Moscheles (1794–1870), and Karl Franz Brendel (1811–68), who had succeeded Schumann as editor of the *Neue Zeitung*. By far the most up-beat of his new encounters, who quickly became a closest friend, was one Julius Otto Grimm (1827–1903). The two amazed everyone with the speed and immediacy with which they shared opinions and inspiration. They became inseparable, together founding the *Kaffernbund*, a 'League of Asses' that even seems to have 'recruited' Joachim. In 1860, Grimm was to become conductor at Münster, a post he held for four decades.

Brahms returned to his home in Hamburg for Christmas, not at all the haphazardly determined figure who had set out months before with Reményi. He was a confident man; he could afford to look with disdain upon cliques and flattery. He knew the scale of the challenge before him – to establish himself as a composer in his own right in the midst of these factions and rivalries. At times his manner came close to arrogance, both to help create as well as to defend this private certainty. Joachim's account of Brahms's ambivalent character, in a letter of late 1854, gives us a glimpse of his abrasive sweep through life:

> *As for Brahms, who put up here on the black sofa for a few days, I did not really feel at ease with him . . . Brahms is egoism incarnate,* without himself being aware of it. *He bubbles over in his cheery way with exuberant thoughtlessness – but sometimes with a lack of consideration (not a lack of reserve, for that would please me!) which offends because it betrays a want of culture. He has never once troubled to consider what others, according to their natures and the course of their development, will hold in esteem; the things that do not arouse* his *enthusiasm, or that do not fit in with* his *experience, or even with* his *mood, are callously thrust aside, or, if he is in the humour, attacked with a malicious sarcasm . . .*
>
> *He knows the weaknesses of the people about him, and he makes use of them, and then does not hesitate to show (to their faces, I admit) that he is crowing over them. His immediate surroundings are quite apart from his musical life, and from his attachment to a higher and more fantastic world. And the way in which he wards off all the morbid emotions and imaginary troubles of others is really delightful. He is absolutely sound in that, just as his complete indifference to the means of existence is beautiful, indeed magnificent.*

Joachim's letter goes on to praise Brahms's piano playing, 'second only to Liszt's' in his experience but, curiously, he calls it cold and passionless. Joachim's style, though, was always 'classical', in comparison to the flappingly Romantic antics of the likes of Reményi. Perhaps the reference was to Brahms's delivery of the *pluies de perles* repertoire, with his disdain seeping through – and not to his performance of his own compositions.

UNHAPPY NEW PATHS

The breezy happiness was not to last. Early in January 1854, Brahms had made his way to Hanover, initially to see Joachim and Grimm; they were soon joined by Robert and Clara Schumann, all to hear Joachim conduct Schumann's *Symphony No.4.*

To begin with, all went well. Brahms's usual dance through the social and musical circles continued in Hanover. There was always momentum to Brahms's cheerfulness and in these months he certainly had the wind in his hair. In particular he met the pianist, conductor and writer Hans von Bülow (1830–94), who remained a significant figure throughout his life. Despite his reserve in accepting Brahms's genius right away, von Bülow gave the first public performance of music by Brahms not played by the composer soon after their meeting, in the March of that year. On this trip Schumann was also in surprisingly fine fettle until the first urgent signs of his madness began to show – signs which, until that point, his friends had ascribed mainly to his excessively poetic disposition.

His moody, rambling spirit, spasmodically in deep, impenetrable solitude, and his sometimes esoteric beliefs, had long given others cause for concern – he was at that time working on a theme he claimed had been dictated to him by the shades of Mendelssohn and Schubert, an unlikely pair in itself. But now, on his return to Düsseldorf, after parting from his other friends, his sanity collapsed. On 27 February, clad only in his dressing-gown, he rose from his desk, left the house and gardens and jumped from a bridge into the Rhine. The crew of a steamer fished him from the water but by then he was incoherent; within days he was taken to an asylum in Endenich, near Bonn, never to leave. He would die there two long years later.

SCHUMANN OFF-STAGE

Brahms joined Clara as quickly as he could and can squarely be credited with holding Clara's life together. He cleared the household of the well-meaning but useless fussers and busybodies. She was then pregnant and for both their sakes was not permitted to see Schumann, whose condition fluctuated, giving the sporadic signs of false hope that so often torture the family more than they relieve the patient.

Brahms, however, visited Schumann quite often. He played duets with him, and Schumann asked for a portrait of Brahms – one that he had had in his study – to be sent to the asylum. On occasions, Brahms was permitted to take Schumann for a walk outside the asylum. They corresponded a great deal as well, Brahms's tactful and cheering letters fine in their precocious maturity. Despite his ramblings, but with imagination and insight, Schumann often wrote to Brahms on the subject of Brahms's music and his pianism. Even in the spring of 1855 Schumann was writing to Joachim to repeat his hope that Brahms would take on writing a Mass, or, at any rate, a work for massed forces such as orchestra and choir – a hope first expressed in his *Neue Zeitung* article.

Brahms's long letter to Clara of 23/24 February 1855 is a joyous as well as a heart-rending document; he describes talking and walking with Schumann, who was always too anxious or frightened to ask the doctors for anything and had thus run out of writing paper. They had played duets and had gone through Brahms's *Sonata* Op.1. Brahms had secured permission for Schumann to accompany him back to the station, which they did by a circuitous route, to prolong the pleasure of the stroll, but a warden always remained in tow. Schumann 'found no difficulty with the well-known Brahms pace which is often too much for you', he told her.

Meanwhile, Clara's child, Felix, was born on 11 June 1854; he was her seventh. Brahms took on the responsibility of looking after the family as much as he could – both emotionally and financially. For some years his publications as well as his concert appearances were few; they were inspired more by consequent financial needs than by relish for the activity. His concert appearances were certainly too few for his admirers and, indeed, too few to capitalize on the publicity Schumann's article had given him. With some insight into his character but none as to what it would become, Anton Rubinstein was to write, 'For the salon he is insufficiently at ease; for the concert hall, not sufficiently fiery; for life in the country, not rough enough; for city life, not sophisticated enough. I have little confidence in such people.'

Schumann's insanity had inspired rumours that rather undermined his recent extravagant advocacy of Brahms. This quite suited Brahms, however, for he was not drawn to what he saw as exhibitionism. If he was to live up to all that Schumann had predicted (and he had little doubt that he could), he wanted to do so in private at his own pace and in public, or in print, only when absolutely sure of himself. Nonetheless, tours took him to Danzig, Hamburg, Altona, Kiel, Bremen and Leipzig. He gave his first performances as soloist with orchestra in Bremen, on 20 November 1855, playing Beethoven's *'Emperor' Concerto*, and later in Leipzig (Beethoven's *Concerto No.4*) and Hamburg (Mozart's *Concerto in D minor*, K.466). In these last two works, Brahms supplied his own cadenzas at the points in the outer movements at which the soloist used to be expected to improvize. Brahms's cadenzas to these and some other concertos survive.

Clara and Brahms supported each other inseparably during what remained of Robert Schumann's life. Their relationship flourished – and some nice exchanges of duty took place: Brahms would quite often perform Schumann's music in his recitals and began the task of sorting and editing Schumann's papers and manuscripts. In October and December 1854, Clara, for her part, gave first performances of Brahms's *Sonata No.3*, Op.5, in Leipzig and Magdeburg, and in 1856 she gave the first ever performance in England of Brahms's music. She played his work often and continued to do so throughout her life: in 1873 she was to rescue his *Piano Concerto No.1* nearly fifteen years after its first unsuccessful performances in Hanover and Leipzig.

Brahms did not publish much but he did work on a great deal of new composition, plunged as he was into the extreme tensions of love and loyalty, hope, counter-hopes and dreads, that inform his greatest music. By 1855 or 1856 he had begun a troubled and troubling *Piano Quartet*, then in C sharp and in piano duet form. Later this haunting piece was to become the *Piano Quartet No.3*, Op.60, which, in its questioning, clenched-fistedly bewildered view of the world, stands at the heart of his creative output. Yet however much his outward life may seem to have withdrawn after Schumann's confinement, it was quite the opposite for his inner life.

Brahms had entered a phase of extraordinarily torn passions

for a young man of even such robust sensitivity as we hear in the sonatas. His endearment to Schumann and his true admiration for the composer's genius meant that he fully shared with Clara all the hopes and the fears for his friend's health – but Clara's strength and perseverance bewitched him, and his fervent admiration grew steadily into love. Brahms was still a young man in his early twenties, carefree in attitude and with a sturdy and at times even tavernish sense of humour – Clara, in her mid-thirties, was, by contrast (and not without reason) a rather serious, troubled person.

THE DEATH OF SCHUMANN

Schumann died in the summer of 1856, on 29 July. Clara and Brahms were with him. He was forty-six. Thereupon, Brahms's relationship with Clara changed. For one thing, she quickly moved to Berlin, without Brahms. Speculation as to just how intimate they had been after Schumann's collapse is more or less futile, and most likely to tell us more about ourselves than about Brahms or Clara. The ever more elaborately amorous language of the letters is no evidence at all if taken in the context of the idiom of the time. Indeed, such language rather suggests a restraint from any form of sexual relationship. What is more, Brahms had been frank in his letters to Schumann as to his devotion to Clara and the joy they shared in friendship, both longing for his return from the asylum. Brahms, it is certain, was not capable of writing such things at all cynically, or with anything less than total sincerity, even to a man in a lunatic asylum.

Throughout his life Brahms understood the ideas of greatness and of gratitude; his legendary gruffness may have sprung from conscience of how far he was destined to go but it was never at the price of an awareness of just how far he had come. The love and creative energy in the Schumann household, so deep-rooted and so generously flowering to Brahms's benefit, could only inspire in such a character a sense of extravagant love in return. If Clara had allowed herself to be Brahms's lover in Schumann's lifetime – and everything about her rather strict character suggests that this was altogether unlikely – such relations certainly ended immediately upon her husband's death.

Even the quantity of their letters, as well as their insistently loving tone, suggest that the act of correspondence was itself the expression of their love. The most likely interpretation was that such passion, liberally expressed in letters and in their chaste togetherness, was awaiting resolution. It is true that the sense of other things being 'on hold' can be pervasive during the final illness of a loved-one; so, too, can a temporary excess of passion seem to provide a much-needed feeling of security. In this case, only Schumann's death could bring the resolution and it was then that Clara and Brahms withdrew rapidly from any further intimacy.

It may be that, for all he had hoped for in this love, the realization of those hopes now filled Brahms with awkward dread. A passage from a letter written to Joachim in the summer of 1854 expresses the dilemma of temptation:

> *Often I must forcibly restrain myself from just quietly putting my arms around her and even – I don't know, it seems to me so natural that she would not take it ill. I think I can no longer love a young girl. At least I have quite forgotten about them. They but promise heaven while Clara reveals it to us.*

The passage says more about Brahms's subsequent blustery bachelorhood than the outcome of his tussle with temptation. He certainly fumbled his relations with women from that time on, and it is conceivable that this was just what he intended. At any rate, whatever damage the relationship did to Brahms's subsequent love-life, he and Clara forged from their intimacy in the shadow of Schumann's madness a bonded friendship that never failed in forty years.

BRAHMS WITHOUT CLARA

Brahms was in turmoil. With Robert Schumann's death he had lost his greatest friend and musical inspiration; in separation from Clara, although he gained an extraordinary friendship, he lost his greatest inspiration as a lover. His direction wavered for a while in the wake of the composer's death, not least because life no longer pivoted around the Schumann household, and he turned to the repertoire of his many friends.

He had good links in many cities – in Hamburg, of course, but also in Düsseldorf, Leipzig and Hanover. But wisely he eventually struck out to new territory, and in September 1857 accepted a post at the court in Detmold. Brahms's application had been promoted by one of his pupils; the post was to last for the four months of the autumn, while the pay was enough to manage on for the whole of the rest of the year.

BRAHMS AT DETMOLD

Just under fifty miles south-west of Hanover but off the main routes of road, railway or river, Detmold lies in the foothills of the various undulating ranges that mark the southern boundary between the flatlands of Northern Germany and the hilly South. Brahms's responsibilities were to take the choir and to play as well as to teach the Princess and others. He found it unstimulating – four months were quite enough, yet it is also plain that Detmold gave him exactly the seclusion and the tranquillity of natural surroundings that would do him good, providing a tonic for all the agitated hopes and ambitions of the preceding years. He allowed his contract to be renewed in the two following years.

The court was an elegant and old-fashioned one. This archaic air gave the perfect calm in which the new Brahms could mature, while his sense of irony could also mature, as he infused his love of form and technique with heart-rending emotion. That elegant environment, with its fancy columns and curly decoration, now helps us to grasp an aspect of Brahms that is all too easily overlooked – his taste for the baroque, for the values of counterpoint and the cleanliness of intricate, sprightly texture not normally associated with the tidal melodies of Romantic music. Not only in their anachronistic title, reminiscent of Mozart, the two *Serenades* for orchestra echo the archaic air; both were written at Detmold.

In these two years (1857–59) Detmold was his home for only a third of the year. The rest of Brahms's time was spent mostly in Hamburg, after a while not in the city itself, with his parents, but in Hamm, a village-like suburb to the east, and not yet engulfed by the city. Little by little, Brahms was distancing himself from his native city. This pendulum of his annual calendar seemed to suit his taste for a balance of contrasts.

Another source of contrast was soon to come into his life: she was Agathe von Siebold, a soprano whom Brahms met while on summer holiday in nearby Göttingen and whose charm not only kept him lingering there outside the holiday period but also inspired the first of his very finest songs, the sets of *Eight Songs and Romances*, Op.14, and of *Five Poems*, Op.19. Indeed, they became engaged – in secret. But when it came to it, Brahms could not face the loss of liberty, nor could he stomach being betrothed to one whose rather better circumstances might have been called upon to help him through what were still difficult times. Temptations too great to resist were often exactly the ones that a nature such as Brahms's found equally too great to accept.

His way of handling this situation may also shed some light on the separation from Clara, for instead of breaking off the engagement, he wrote a letter to Agathe that at one level plainly declared his love but at another also seemed to issue an ultimatum. 'I love you! I must see you again! – but I cannot wear fetters. Write to me whether I am to come back, to take you in my arms.' This indecisive bluster did not impress Agathe and she broke off the relationship.

For a second time Brahms had managed to combine a rush of passion with a timely escape. This duality within his character becomes ever more obvious. He was able to control the balance between his unhappy state of mind and second-rate behaviour on the one hand, and happily creative freedom on the other – a creative freedom that also included the paradoxical but important freedom to experience failure and unhappiness. He later wrote to a friend:

> *When I should have liked to marry, my music was either hissed in the concert halls or received with only icy coldness. Now for myself I could bear that well enough because I knew its value; I knew that one day the tables would be turned. What's more, when I came home after such failures I was not unhappy. On the contrary. But if at such moments I had had to meet the anxious, questioning eyes of a wife with the words 'another failure', I could not have borne that. And if she had wanted to comfort me for my failure, argh! I cannot think what a hell that would have been. . . .*

From this period of balanced contrasts on so many levels emerged not just chamber music of rural energy but also that vast, steel-hulled steamship of a piece, the *Piano Concerto No.1*.

CHAPTER 4
FROM DETMOLD
TO HAMBURG
(1857–62)

- ♦ *The First Piano Concerto*
- ♦ *The 'Manifesto'*
- ♦ *Brahms, Wagner and Opera*
- ♦ *Snubbed by Hamburg*

The *Piano Concerto* had been through all sorts of twists and transformations that now shed interesting light upon Brahms's way of handling his material. It had started as a sonata for two pianos; then it became a symphony, and only then all of a sudden in February 1855 could he write to Clara: 'Just think what I dreamed last night: I used my symphony that came to grief, as a piano concerto!'

That, of course, was only the beginning of yet more work. The third movement proved especially problematic. Only in Beethoven's *'Emperor' Concerto* had a composer set himself anything like so hard a task of balancing the frantic dance of the last movement against the momentum of the energies unleashed in the two earlier movements. Both concertos have distinctly hymn-like middle movements; indeed, in Joachim's copy, Brahms annotated his theme with the text: *Benedictus qui venit in nomine Domini* (Blessed is he who comes in the name of the Lord) – 'Mynheer Domine' had been their nickname for Schumann. Tovey described the movement as a 'Requiem for Schumann'. Later, Brahms told Clara it was meant as a lovely portrait of her.

The concerto is not without bluff and bluster, and is useful as an illustration of Brahms's disingenuous but ingenious way of handling things in general – not only his love-life. In much the same vein, Joachim wrote at about this time that, 'Brahms has a dual personality: one is mostly naive genius . . . the other is one of devilish cunning which, with a frosty surface, suddenly explodes in a pedantic, prosaic need to dominate.' The apparent imbalance of weight in the exchanges that develop between piano pitted against large orchestra towards the close of the first movement can seem to be one of Brahms's early, inexperienced miscalculations of sheer noise – unless they are played with that eye on bluff or rhetoric, as if one side of a personality is 'trying it on' with the other. This alone requires almost more creative understanding and controlled imagination between pianist, conductor and players than in any other concerto in the repertoire.

The first performance took place in Hamburg, after his second term at Detmold, on 22 January 1859, with Brahms as soloist and Joachim at the helm. The reception was cool. It fared even less well a few days later, in Leipzig, at a second performance that was actually hissed; and scarcely better in March, in the composer's home town of Hamburg, this time under one Julius Rietz (1812–77), who was later known for editing the complete Mendelssohn edition. If Brahms had a taste for balance, this was it: a promising early start such as any composer would dream of, publicly urged on to bigger things by the revered Schumann of all people, and a resounding, unanimous flop with his first big composition.

Ever since Schumann's article, Brahms had both benefited and suffered from the expectations that it had aroused. It had brought him to the attention of the public, to be sure, but it also had the effect of unnerving him slightly. He reluctantly took up Schumann's challenge to write something substantial for choral forces; a *Kyrie*, for four-part mixed choir & continuo, as well as five movements for a projected *Mass* for four- and six-part mixed choir have survived – both date from around 1855, but received no public exposure until their publication in 1984. Then, in 1856/57 he also edited Schumann's *Cantata* for voices, choir & orchestra, Op.140, in tidying and correcting the manuscript for publication, an act of homage that doubtless served equally as research.

Now that he had been buffeted by the lacklustre fate of his first big orchestral piece, it was time to take stock.

BELIEFS AND BLUNDERS

The public failure of his concerto made him retreat a little, but it also served to harden his exterior. Brahms was gaining a reputation as someone not quite perfectly presentable on account of his lapses of etiquette in manners and dress. The earliest photographs show fine features, which we forget alongside the later image of bearded corpulence, yet heavy-handedness had set in early – something akin to ham-fistedness had appeared, not only in his playing, by all accounts, but also in his behaviour.

One incident in particular stands out – although out of character to the Brahms we know in overall perspective, it was quite in character at this tricky stage. It is as though, in his need to define himself, a valve burst, and Brahms issued what would nowadays be called 'a statement', or manifesto, attacking the 'New German' school. For a moment Brahms failed to rise above the factions that beset the musical world. He was fortunate that his own genius, and the existence of Schumann's support, had given him a position ever so slightly above the fray, and some of the antagonism towards Brahms was based more on such anecdotes as his dozing off during Liszt's playing, than on his own musical creed. Nonetheless, the valve burst.

It all seems so bizarre and schoolboyish now, that we might wish they had all just 'got on with it'. Already in 1857 Joachim had written a charmingly portentous letter to Liszt to announce his formal breaking-off of support. It opened in tones of mutual self-congratulation steeped in flattery, but went on to state, with sudden directness: 'Your music is entirely antagonistic to me; it contradicts everything with which the spirits of our great ones have nourished my mind from my earliest youth.' Ah!

At any rate, the *Neue Zeitschrift* had also become uncomfortably partisan since Schumann's days as editor. True, it had been conceived by Schumann as part of what he styled the 'Band of David's March on the Philistines' – in essence the voice of the New against the stodgy traditionalists of the Old – but this cheery campaigning tone had been stepped-up by his successor Paul Brendel, to support the New German school. Brahms did not like this. He was also unhappy that, for the celebrations of its quarter-century, the *Neue Zeitschrift* had omitted to invite Clara, let alone himself or Joachim. All the same, to be fair, Brendel had followed Schumann's eulogistic article up with some of the most sympathetic criticism of Brahms's subsequent output, and no paper was kinder about the *First Piano Concerto*.

By 1860, however, Brahms had become so unnerved by all this appearance of jealousy, rivalry and conflict that he persuaded Joachim to join him in writing a 'musical creed', in fact an attack on the aims of the New German school, especially its claim to be the only way forward for German art. Along with Clara Schumann, Joachim and a few others, and with a certain degree of reluctance, Brahms had come to represent the opposing 'school'. The very phrase 'musical creed' seems out of character with Brahms all the same; he had none of Wagner's relish for long-sentenced, jargon-filled bombast.

Not surprisingly then, the Brahms 'Manifesto' was delight-fully clumsy:

> *The undersigned declare that so far at least as they are concerned, the principles stated by Brendel's journal are not recognized, and that they regard the productions of the leaders and pupils of the so-called 'New-German' school, which in part simply reinforce these principles in practice and in part again enforce new and unheard-of theories, as contrary to the innermost spirit of music, strongly to be deplored and condemned.*

. . . and so on.

It appeared in the Berlin *Echo*, signed by Brahms and Joachim and with an unconvincing total of only two other signatures. (In his biography, Niemann's kinder version of things is that the letter was still in circulation, to gather signatures, when the *Echo* published it adventitiously with only the original four.) It had little effect except to make a laughing-stock of the four of them for a short while, although it had given Wagner an opportunity for one of the earliest of his prose outbursts of equally silly anger and spite.

BRAHMS AND WAGNER

The relationship between Brahms and Wagner over the years is interesting. It may be thought that two composers whose output did not overlap could have stood above questions of rivalry but, while each was ultimately too musical not to admire the other professionally, they were both too bloody-minded to let it show.

The two composers had similarities – albeit superficial – from the supposedly Saxon shape of their heads (one image of Brahms's head in the 1860s, before he grew his beard, could be used as an image of Wagner were he not ever so slightly too podgy around the jowls) to their political hopes for German unification.

The main similarity between them, however, is a strong one – strong enough to have kept them at least at arm's length from each other as rivals in history – for each took upon himself the follow-through of Beethoven's challenge. Brahms adhered to sonata form and instrumental music, taking his lead, it might be said, from the Beethoven of the *'Hammerklavier' Sonata*, while Wagner took his cue from the Beethoven epitomized by the last movement of the *Symphony No.9*, the *'Choral'*. He believed that every avenue of instrumental music had been thoroughly exhausted and that the only real way forward lay in the ultimate marriage of music and words – in 'Music-Drama'.

So, Brahms's relationship with Wagner had always been distant; the 'Manifesto' now kept them well apart. There was, all the same, an odd exchange between them in the summer of 1875, which might have opened into more cordial relations. It all harks back to 1862–63, when Brahms, the Polish virtuoso Carl Tausig (1841–71), Peter Cornelius and others had helped prepare the orchestral parts for Wagner's concerts in Vienna. Wagner had ever since kept in his mind an image of what he described as 'the lean Brahms who had corrected instrumental parts for him in Vienna, and whom he had then rediscovered 'fattened up' by fame.' However, more than a decade later he wished to have back a manuscript of the so-called *'Venusberg'* music (written specially for performances of *Tannhäuser* in Paris), which Brahms had acquired as a gift from Tausig. Accordingly, in June 1875, Wagner wrote to Brahms to ask for it.

Now Tausig had never actually owned it, let alone ever had the right to give it away. Matching wrong for wrong, Brahms had, a little mischievously, held onto it. Now that Wagner needed it for a new edition of the opera, he had to write to Brahms, a letter certainly full of disingenuous *politesse*, signed 'your most respectful and obedient servant', the most flowery of his formalities. He dreaded that Brahms might hold onto his ill-gotten treasure. Brahms, however, responded by sending it to him immediately, asking in return for a full score of *Die Meistersinger*; Wagner had none left and sent him a less useful but nevertheless fancily-bound edition of *Das Rheingold*.

This was not exactly a snub, even if it cuts it fine. Cosima Wagner noted in her diary that Wagner received a 'strangely sagacious letter' of thanks. Sagacity from Brahms surprised the Wagners: a year before, she had noted in her *Diaries* a conversation 'about Herr Brahms and his damaging and bigoted influence on the educated middle classes.' Given that Wagner once said that Brahms composed 'as Bach might have composed', a glimmer of understanding and respect filters through, all the same, but on the other hand, Nietzsche once observed Wagner throw Brahms's music to the floor in an enraged envy. 'At that moment, Wagner,' he remarked sadly, 'was not great.'

Brahms's dealings with other composers were usually open, whether in admiration, respect or sheer dislike. He made no bones about such things, even about his enthusiasm for certain of Wagner's operas. He was capable of giving the highest compliment too: he delighted to tell Johann Strauss that he would give everything he had composed to have written the *Blue Danube Waltz*, writing under the title of a copy of the piece, 'Not, alas, by Johannes Brahms.' Equally, upon hearing of the death of Wagner (in February 1888), Brahms halted a rehearsal to announce the loss of a 'master', and did not resume work until the next day.

BRAHMS, OPERA AND SONG

The fact that Brahms wrote no opera cannot be used to dismiss Brahms as an 'abstract' composer (as Wagner did), because with Brahms, song is of such vital importance. (One or two of his piano pieces and chamber music even have texts above them – a practice associated with Schumann.) In his songs, moreover, he takes musical 'picture-painting' to far more painterly heights than Schumann or Schubert ever did and in a way that was a model to Hugo Wolf, despite their personal antipathy.

Brahms began to write for voices at the very beginning of his career, first songs and then music for choirs. He enjoyed writing for choral groups; in particular there had been the Detmold choir, as well as a group he started to assemble in Hamburg. Whereas he sometimes worked more on orchestral music than on piano music, or vice versa, he worked on songs continuously throughout his life. Despite his antipathy to 'programme' music (instrumental music intended to depict the events and characters of a story, or to describe a landscape, without words), it is in his songs that we now see his power as a painter of musical pictures – the song '*Ständchen*', Op.106, No.1, a setting of a Kugler '*Serenade*', perfectly paints in a couple of strokes the moonlit carousal of students serenading a young girl. And it is in the songs, too, that we perceive Brahms's understanding of drama. Brahms had a particularly happy knack of conveying a relationship between two people with but one voice: excellent examples of this are found in '*Von ewiger Liebe*' ('Eternal Love'; Op.43, No.1) and '*Wir wandelten*' ('We used to wander'; Op.96, No.2).

As for opera itself, the challenge laid down by Beethoven was as serious as that of sonata. Beethoven had written only one opera and that was *Fidelio* – a unique piece in which the opera takes both its old *Singspiel* form, the use of spoken word and song in alternation, as well as its full-blown continuous musical form, and trounces both, the whole culminating in an unprecedented moral intensity. For many people it is the greatest opera ever written, and for many others the most ungainly. It may be both! Whichever is the case, *Fidelio* was as hard an act to follow as the '*Hammerklavier*' *Sonata*.

As far as traditions went, the rather less serious genre of Italian opera could carry on undeterred by Beethoven's example, but in the German repertoire there was pandemonium, filled for a while by such stopgaps as the 'dramatic cantata'. Schubert floundered between these forms, as did Schumann; Brahms wrote one such cantata, *Rinaldo*, to a text by Goethe, and no opera. *Rinaldo* is operatic enough in subject – the dilemma between duty and love – but Brahms's treatment is not operatic; he seeks squarely to add to the Romantic cantata repertoire. His dramatic gift was for the cameo world of song, not for the grand gestures of heroes – the one thing the '*Tragic*' *Overture* of 1881 is not, is tragic. The German opera tradition was only safe once Wagner had sorted the picture out with innovative resolve, creating an unprecedented scale of drama and music that looks back only to Beethoven or Shakespeare.

Nevertheless, Brahms must have played with the idea of producing an opera, for he even went so far as to advertise for a libretto that might be suitable; but he found none. At one time a libretto had been produced from the same source of fables as had yielded Mozart's *The Magic Flute*, but to no avail. We know from his friends that Brahms was in general uneasy at the idea of continuous music through a drama. He preferred the *Singspiel*, which had reached its heights in *The Magic Flute*, or, for that matter, in *Fidelio*, but even so, the fable failed to sustain his enthusiasm.

One subject he toyed with (in conversation at any rate if not actually in music) was 'a grotesque and extravagant farce', with magical transformations and so on. This might have brought from him an exceptionally rich score, for the grotesque is an aspect of the instrumental palette that unfortunately few performers have the nerve to explore; but regrettably this project was also allowed to lapse.

THE SYMPHONIST IN WAITING

Brahms had moved to the rural atmosphere of Hamm, at least partly to compensate for the decision in 1860 not to remain in his post at Detmold. Away from the bustle of Hamburg, he could carry on working away with as little disturbance as possible. In Hamm, his lodging was with the widow of one Dr. Rösing and she took part in a small ladies' choir that interested Brahms and for which Brahms had originally invented the light-heartedly earnest tag, *Fix oder Nix*.

The list of his works shows how seriously he took the simultaneous need both to consolidate and to explore. Part of this process included scholarly work sometimes overlooked as an aspect of his character. For instance, he edited six concertos for keyboard with string quartet by C.P.E. Bach (published in 1862) – not an obvious choice in those days but a sign of the serious musicological skills that underpinned his Romanticism. Later, in the same vein, he edited or arranged two violin sonatas also by C.P.E. Bach, a sonata for two claviers by W.F. Bach, and twelve *Ländler* by Schubert, all issued in 1864, and two books of *Keyboard Pieces* by Couperin, issued in 1871.

By 1860 he had also met 'Fritz' Simrock, the publisher, who became one of his closest and most trusted friends as well as one of his regular companions on walking holidays. This was Friedrich August Simrock (1837–1901), son of the Peter Joseph Simrock (1792–1868) who had already acquired some of Brahms's early pieces. The publishing house had been started in Bonn by Fritz's grandfather and had had a close association with Beethoven.

Brahms later saw to it that they took on Dvořák.

Fritz was to become custodian of Brahms's money. This itself provides an example of Brahms's characteristic way of avoiding having to handle things himself. In 1877 Brahms explained to Clara that there were two people each with charge of half his money, one of whom had a steel box containing papers; 'and every New Year he sends me an account, which I sign, without, of course, reading or understanding a syllable of it.' He transferred all his funds to Simrock and benefited from the man's financial acumen.

Consciously or not, there was, however, a special subtext to the decision to remain in or around Hamburg: the conductor of the Hamburg Philharmonic Society was not a young man, but one on the verge of retirement. In his desultory but secretly determined way, Brahms let it be no secret that he hoped to win the succession. Eventually the new appointment was made, in the autumn of 1862, but Brahms was not chosen. The post went to the baritone Julius Stockhausen (1826–1906), one of Brahms's best interpreters, whom he had met just before Schumann's death and with whom he gave many recitals both before and after this episode. Stockhausen was not particularly known as a conductor and his selection may have been more a vote against the off-handedly cocky Brahms than a positive vote for Stockhausen. Even when the post became vacant again a few years later, Brahms was passed over. He was clearly nowhere near humble enough to satisfy his home town's equally stubborn pride.

Almost immediately, keen to take his mind off this disappointment, Brahms set off for Vienna with all the relish and anticipation of any musician on a first visit to that city of all cities in the musical world – he went to Vienna. To all intents and purposes he never returned.

CHAPTER 5

THE VIENNESE MASTER AND THE 'GERMAN' REQUIEM
(1863–69)

- ♦ Settling in Vienna
- ♦ Brahms and Hanslick
- ♦ Death of his mother
- ♦ Travels and friends
- ♦ The 'German' Requiem

Wien, Wien, nur du allein! – 'Vienna, Vienna, only you alone!' – the words of the old song matched Brahms's mood once he reached the city that had been home to Mozart, Beethoven, Haydn and Schubert. (It was also a city Wagner had never conquered!) Vienna was a city of carefree seriousness with a delight in irony and opposites, matching the contrasts of Brahms's character. His progression to Vienna was a natural consolidation both of his character as a man and of his choice of the tradition to which he belonged: his music was at home here, as he himself was too.

Brahms already had friends and contacts and he wasted no time settling in. In November 1862, within only two months of his arrival, both his newly completed *Piano Quartets* (Opp.25 & 26) had been given their first public performances, with Brahms himself at the piano. The string players were members of the Hellmesberger Quartet, at the time Vienna's finest, led by Joseph Hellmesberger Snr. (1828–93), professor of violin at the Conservatory and *Konzertmeister* of the Vienna Philharmonic Orchestra as well as of the Court Opera. The Viennese certainly had an appetite for music: at the second of the concerts, in addition to the *Piano Quartet* No.2 Brahms played his own *Piano Sonata*, Op.5, the Handel *Variations and Fugue*, Op.24, as well as a *Toccata* by Bach and Schumann's *Fantasy*, Op.17; there were some of his songs, too, and one Professor Förchtgott played the *Ballades*, Op.10.

At this concert, Brahms also made the acquaintance of Eduard Hanslick (1825–1904), a man who had become the archetype of the self-important critic, apparently powerful enough to rule his corner of the musical world through his newspaper – as critics can do and have done ever since. He immediately encouraged Brahms to give another recital, in January 1863 – a rare occasion in that both Wagner and Hanslick attended. Hanslick's was the leading voice against Wagner and so he has gone into history as an object of ridicule: the man who was so very wrong about Wagner. He had been the subject of Wagner's mimicry in *Die Meistersinger* (the character Beckmesser ridicules the pedantry of critics), which had just been given a private performance in Vienna that year. Yet he was an honest and sincere man, convinced of the importance of music and musicians. Brahms had no illusions about Hanslick's limitations, but neither did he fail to appreciate Hanslick's importance in Vienna; they remained good friends.

After this first successful season in Vienna, Brahms returned to Hamburg, in the summer of 1863, having already been offered the post of director of the *Singakademie* in Vienna with effect from the following September. After considerable vacillation – for it would mean a very definite break of ties with his native city – he accepted.

In his letter of acceptance, quite apart from acknowledging the honour, he remarked a shade disingenuously or perhaps premeditatedly, upon the gravity of a decision to give up his freedom 'for the first time'. The job did at any rate give him a way of cocking a snook at Hamburg for failing to appoint him to the Philharmonic Orchestra, as well as a handy pretext for allowing the evident lure of Vienna to sway him back.

The *Singakademie* was not, however, an altogether happy appointment. His choice of repertoire was fresh, working as he did on the then still unusual Bach cantatas as well as pieces by Beethoven and Schubert – the last of the season's concerts was an all-Brahms programme – but the singers were taxed beyond their capacities. The demands exacted of the singers by his '*Fix oder Nix'* attitude proved his undoing and the later concerts were not an overall success. He was offered a renewed contract for a further three years but he felt more comfortable leaving the post after that first season, and in May 1864 he resigned.

Yet another of Brahms's not entirely successful relationships waxed – and waned again – during this Vienna season, when he met and was bowled over by one Ottolie Hauer, a singer who had shown herself to be a fine interpreter of his songs. Bluster, dither and passion buffeted against one another within him and it was probably with some relief that he found, when he eventually proposed to her on Christmas Day, that she had accepted another man only hours before. Brahms was off the hook and not too displeased by the fact. It makes little odds whether he had managed to go so far without any idea of another suitor's existence or whether he had known perfectly well that she was already receiving the attentions of another man: either way, his trepidatious and half-hearted approach to affairs of the heart are now all too evident.

He returned to Hamburg again for the summer of 1864. By a curious irony, Julius Stockhausen had now appointed Brahms's father to the Philharmonic, as a double-bass player. Still, the family household was not in a good state. His father had to practise more than before and, even confined to the attic, drove everyone to their wits' end. The strain drove his parents to separate and Brahms took on most of the emotional as well as the financial burden of this upheaval, returning to Vienna for the winter start to the season in a reflective but not unthankful mood. Neither Hamburg nor matrimony had trapped him.

Already his annual routine had been established. Brahms liked his life well-ordered – just as he always liked to rise early and start his day with strong coffee and end it with good beer or wine. The 'season' began in the autumn and ended in late spring, and during these months Brahms lived and worked in Vienna. In the summer came holidays and trips to resorts, towns and cities throughout the German-speaking areas of Europe, all organized to take in friends at every stop.

He worked on composition all the time. For instance, in the New Year 1865 he finished the *Waltzes* for piano duet. These he cunningly dedicated to Hanslick – cunningly, given that their popular success was assured and so Hanslick, still not entirely convinced by Brahms, could be flattered without having to engage in any critical thinking whatsoever. The waltzes had another context: of mischief, as well as professional envy and admiration, for it had been in the summer of 1864 that Brahms had met the 'Waltz King', Johann Strauss II (1825–99), recently appointed Conductor of the Court Balls. Brahms admired his music just as much as he relished to be in the company of the great *bon vivant*. They got on well and became good friends. A set of Viennese waltzes was therefore a slightly cheeky but also confident publication in the city that was clearly now to be his home.

DEATH OF HIS MOTHER

It was early in February 1865 that Brahms received news of his mother's last illness. He set off immediately but reached Hamburg too late to see her alive: she had died quickly, in less than twelve hours. Stockhausen was one of the crowd that followed the old woman's coffin to her grave and Brahms was touched by the entire occasion.

He wrote a letter to Clara in which there is little evidence of his pain, so concerned was he with an injury to Clara's right hand that she had sustained a whole month before, and with his sister's state of mind – Elise had been with their mother throughout her sudden and unexpected demise. Clara's reply explains some of this restraint – she speaks of his having to 'suffer the sorrow which you have dreaded so long.' She, too, was worried about Elise, but as it was, within a week of the funeral, Brahms had been driven from Hamburg by his sister's anxious temper and he clearly felt himself to be in the way. Again he wrote to Clara, mentioning his mother's age in brackets for the second letter in succession – indeed almost with a sense of foreboding of his own shorter life-span:

> *Time changes everything for better or for worse. It does not so much change as it builds up and develops, and thus when once this sad year is over I shall begin to miss my dear good mother ever more and more. I cannot write any more about it. The one comforting feature about our loss is that it ended a relationship which really could only have become sadder with the years, and at least I can thank heaven that it kept my mother as long as it did (seventy-six years) and let her go so peacefully.*

Brahms's father remarried in March 1866. Brahms contained his sorrow and set off afresh with unfettered vigour, though his music after his mother's death does reflect an ever richer palette of dark shades in his life.

He began to travel far more than before – to Switzerland, Holland, Denmark, remaining within more-or-less German-speaking territory. It was another ten years before Brahms was to 'discover' Italy. Often, after his mother's death, his trips would include a spell in the company of his father, who had seldom ever had the money to leave Hamburg. They were two different but equally two similar sorts, each proud of the other, and their new relationship was a happy one, as was Brahms's relationship with his father's new wife.

In each of these countries he built up that repertoire of friends and walking companions that round out his life story. Much documented detail remains of their elaborate itineraries, Brahms's path criss-crossing with that of his friends around a number of North European holiday spots and concert venues.

There was Levi in Karlsruhe, Deiters in Bonn, Billroth and the Wesendoncks in Zürich, and Rieter-Biedermann in Winterthur; then there was Dietrich at Oldenburg, Reinthaler in Bremen, and, of course, Clara in Berlin. At one time he even came close to living in Zürich, especially under the influence of the Wesendonk family – who had, some time previously, been hosts to Wagner.

At every stopping-place there were favourite friends – and a piano: Brahms's life was, we can now see, a celebration of the rapid advances made in two Victorian technologies – the piano and the railways – since some of the rhythmic and emotive momentum of his music and its unleashed power might have been inspired by his beloved railways. The characteristic tempi of his music suggest with ever more deft rhythmic control the emotional patterns of travel – by train as well as strolling and walking, trotting or cantering. Perhaps even the jolts of the *Piano Quartet No.3*, Op.60, whatever the tragic impact that they have, come from the thrill of premonition felt as your train is shunted and the engine changed.

Brahms described in a letter once, with impressive matter-of-fact tone, how Joachim was involved in a head-on train collision in which his only injuries were a bang on the head sustained by his violin falling from the luggage rack above his head.

His fewer and fewer public performances on these trips became events of a special kind. Although he had started his career as a virtuoso, he had never been flashily so and by now, with his reputation assured and his youth no longer part of the spectacle, he could relax a little. He did – indeed, he became known for slapdash execution reminiscent of the great pianist Artur Schnabel.

That, in turn, prompts a pair of kindred anecdotes. Brahms played the Schumann *Piano Concerto* at a concert in the mid-1860s, and at an exposed exchange of melodies with the oboe he heard the player make a mistake in the tune. Brahms thereupon repeated the wrong phrase, in his turn, effectively disguising the error and holding things together. Something similar happened to the characterful conductor Sir Hamilton Harty in the 1930s, with Schnabel at the piano, in a performance of Brahms's *Second Concerto*. Schnabel skipped two bars in the last movement but Harty deftly signalled to the orchestra in such a way as to make invisible amends. In good spirits after the concert, Schnabel said to Harty that his Hallé Orchestra was 'almost as good as the Berlin Philharmonic', to which the laconic Irishman replied, 'You don't say? I think they are two bars better even.'

At the time of his mother's death, Brahms's perspective had not only shifted towards Vienna, but in new composition he had turned away from the piano. Although he composed no specific works for piano solo, he did edit a quantity of Schubert's most Viennese and folky pieces: forty *Ländler* for piano and for piano duet, as well as the unusual set of three *Impromptus* or *Klavierstücke*, D.946, and Schumann's *Études Symphoniques* (Opp.13 & post.). Moreover, much of his own music was issued in duet arrangements that he himself made, including the first two *Piano Quartets* and the *Piano Quintet* and the first two *String Quartets*. Even the *Requiem*, the completion of which became a priority after the death of his mother, was issued also in piano duet form.

Brahms turned now to chamber music more and more, replacing the bravado of his early piano music with the values of homely music-making. When he later returned to writing for the piano, in the 1890s, the music had taken an unprecedented, solitary feeling. All the same, his chamber music was now composed on a grander scale than before. In particular, the *Piano*

Quartets and *Quintet* demonstrate this. By now, it was as though he had wider streets to stroll, higher hills to walk. Brahms was in his stride.

THE 'GERMAN' REQUIEM

It is at this point that Brahms tackled music of a greater scale than ever before, and beside which even the *Piano Concerto No.1* seems compact. So, though he composed no piano music for many years, after 1865, he did complete or compose two symphonies, two concertos, his only three string quartets, the third piano quartet – and, first of all, the *'German' Requiem*.

In his earliest piano music, conceived on the grand scale, Brahms still did not have a total grasp on the scale. Despite his extraordinary sense of invention, many ideas were left tantalizingly underdeveloped. Moreover, sets of variations, which were his preferred form for extended piano pieces after the three sonatas, do not usually aspire to scale in the same manner by virtue of their 'bittiness': with them he achieved size rather than scale. The *'German' Requiem* was an altogether different matter, not only in length but by being almost entirely slow music. It had taken an enormous amount of effort and was the result of years of sketches and discards; with all its different types of paper and ink, each dating from different periods, the manuscript resembles a seismologist's diagram, with layer upon layer of inspiration and revision.

Two false suppositions about the *Requiem* need to be scotched at this point. The work was definitely not conceived as a tribute to Brahms's mother; its gestation dates much farther back into Brahms's life than that, even if her death may have hastened the piece to the top of the pile. Nor is the use of the word 'German' in the title to be taken as a nationalist manifesto, a supposition often made because of Brahms's antipathy to 'New-German' art. The title simply refers to the language of the text, which is German rather than Latin.

The question of German nationalism is contentious, all the same. Political union of all the little German states was an ambition shared by almost all their inhabitants. Poets, artists and musicians were no exception. It may be surprising to find Brahms's name dragged into this, but he, too, hoped for a unified Germany, and indeed wrote a patriotic hymn to that effect, the

Triumphlied, written in 1870–71 to mark the German triumphs over France in 1870. Wagner's sentiments were the same.

However, Wagner also poured out a deluge of political ranting in prose and has since been seen to epitomize all the worst of the nationalistic instincts. Thomas Mann, no unequivocal admirer of the 'old wizard', wrote in the 1930s of Wagner's music that 'although he is capable of sounding a folksy German note from time to time for purposes of characterization, as in *Die Meister-singer* and *Siegfried*, this never constitutes the . . . starting point of his musical writing – it is never the *source* from which it wells up spontaneously, as in the work of Schumann, Schubert and Brahms.' It did not take long for Brahms to feel uncomfortable if his *Triumphlied* were played too often.

To return to the *Requiem*. On 1 December 1867, in Vienna, the first three movements alone were performed – an inadequate performance and not a complete success. Hanslick's enthusiasm was tempered by his sensation that the third movement reminded him of the din of a train, a problem in fact caused by a blundering and over-enthusiastic timpanist. The following Easter, Brahms himself conducted a performance in Bremen that lacked only what is now the fourth movement; Stockhausen was the baritone soloist and the piece was received with acclaim. This success set the seal upon Brahms's growing reputation and ensured his truly international celebrity. The remaining movement, for soprano, was completed in May that year, but was kept under wraps until a performance of the full six movements in Leipzig the following February.

The text is taken from Luther's rendering of the Old Testament. The choice of texts and language, although not political, was certainly theological. Brahms was no believer, and this choice can be seen to have been an attempt to satisfy psychological and artistic needs in coping with bereavement in a way more immediately emotional than plainly Christian. Later it was Dvořák who most bluntly expressed the bizarre fact of Brahms's religious beliefs, in the year before Brahms's death: 'Such a man, such a fine soul, yet he doesn't believe in anything, he doesn't believe in anything.'

Brahms remained an atheist throughout his life. Even within his chosen texts for the *Requiem*, he has suppressed passages that make excessively explicit Christian reference. He once remarked that the characters 'are not heathen enough for me in the Bible.' Yet for all that, at no time did the piece have so much as a trace of the theatricality of Verdi's *Requiem*, a work by contrast so decorative that to talk of sincerity, let alone of theological nicety, seems almost ridiculous. Let it be understood that Brahms was an atheist – but a Protestant atheist.

Europe represented a wide market for large-scale choral pieces and Brahms went on to capitalize on this by producing a huge output of choral music, for a while publishing scarcely any chamber music. Especially in England, choral music was as sure a means of creating a market as chamber music or the symphonic repertoire. *Rinaldo*, his not-entirely-satisfactory cantata, and the *Alto Rhapsody*, both date from the years immediately following the success of the *Requiem*, as does the *Song of Destiny*. Brahms became an international figure. However much the *Requiem* brought him fame and fortune, it also propagated the view that his music is irretrievably lugubrious.

CHAPTER 6

FAME AND FORTUNE; HOME AND HABITS IN VIENNA

(the 1870s)

- ♦ *Success of the Requiem*
- ♦ *Brahms's mature character*
- ♦ *Death of his father*
- ♦ *The first two symphonies*

Fame and fortune (Brahms hated the first and was judicious and generous with the second) prompted him also to take an apartment in Vienna that was to become his fixed home there from late 1871 onwards. He had been moving about a lot between the various trips away, from one quaint old address to another; now he was settled.

These rooms were simple enough, on the third floor of No.4 Karlsgasse, serviced by a landlady. From photographs we know that he liked a feeling of space in his rooms. There were few rugs on the floor; the chairs were bentwood ones, more typical of a tavern than the study of a great man, although there was also a leather sofa and a rocking chair sometimes poised forward to spill an unwary visitor. In his main room, the piano was tucked against the window wall, with an outsize bust of Beethoven threateningly lodged on a plinth above the player's head. At first he owned Schumann's piano, and later a Streicher, as well as a 'square' piano that had supposedly belonged to Haydn. (For public concerts he preferred a Bechstein.) His bedroom looked out over a rambling garden with a walnut tree – exactly the sort to be found 'by the front door' in a celebrated Schumann song, *Der Nußbaum*.

Brahms was a collector – his acquisitions numbered old

books, manuscripts and music as well as an array of tin soldiers. Brahms was very fond of 'old favourites' and did not lightly discard his possessions. Right back in his earliest days in Vienna, and even after his financial worries had disappeared, he was known for his shabby old clothes and disordered dress-sense. In his youth he wore the sort of top-hat that looks perpetually too small and in danger of falling off; had he gone to the United States on that impresario's offer, he would have looked the part selling medicine from a covered wagon. The hat he took on his walks was not so much for his head but an increasingly decrepit accessory for his hands to fiddle with. In 1855 he had already found that he could amuse Schumann, then in the asylum, with his 'Hungarian' hat. And at the first performance of the *Violin Concerto* in 1879, his trousers, held up by an old tie, nearly came down.

Contemporary drawings and Viennese cartoons depict Brahms, as often as not, walking or striding rather than conducting. There is almost a foretaste of Winnie-the-Pooh about them; one famous sequence of sketches of his conducting shows him at one moment with his lorgnettes flapping at his belly, at another his left hand resting in his trouser pocket. A nice touch in early editions of the *Oxford Companion to Music* is the charmingly maladroit drawing for the entry on Brahms, by 'Batt', showing him not in full flow at desk or keyboard, or on a walk, but engaged in the ritual tinkering with his morning coffee apparatus, the day's first cigar already half-smoked.

Brahms enjoyed a good practical joke (as did Bismarck!) and he acquired a reputation for that as well as for his capacity for frank rudeness. He also possessed a sharp, quick wit, of the sort nowadays associated with the conductor Sir Thomas Beecham. Stories abound, as when a cellist, complaining of Brahms's loud playing, said that he could hardly hear himself play, to which Brahms replied, 'He should be so lucky!' But Brahms was aware of this reputation and could turn his wit to a charming, almost apologetic self-deprecation, as when he left a gathering with the words, 'If there is anyone here I have failed to insult, I beg their pardon.'

Sometimes, however, his verbal gaucherie was genuinely inadvertent and gave cause for regret. On tour in Denmark with Joachim just after the 1864 war, Brahms casually expressed a wish that their national art collection were in Berlin – this was immediately taken the wrong way, and was reported in the morning papers. It is, of course, likely that Brahms simply meant that it would be so much more convenient for him to visit this collection, which pleased him so well, if it were located in Berlin, rather than as a regret that the collection had not become German spoils of war. However, the Danes took the latter meaning, the scandal was instantaneous and Brahms took the train out of the country the next day.

BRAHMS ALONE

He remained a bachelor throughout his life. Time and time again in his encounters with women, over-cautiousness and hesitation would prompt either a blustering attempt at resolution, or a quick escape. He was even known to remark, of women, that 'None of them would have me; and if there had been one who would, I could not have stood her on account of her bad taste.' Even so, he always regretted not having a family of his own children, and he adored the children of others. In Vienna, for instance, his landlady's children were habitually spoilt by Brahms, who, for his part, enjoyed being called 'Onkel B'.

Brahms was often lonely, but he was not often alone. He hated to take a holiday by himself and his trips were rarely organized without a supporting cast of male friends at the various watering-holes, ready to talk and play music, to walk mountains, to explore forests, to share in food and drink and to have a 'jolly good time'. The rumbustious, sing-song mood of the *Academic Festival' Overture*, its arms-entwined exuberance so perfectly expressed, is not lightly to be dismissed, for it is good evidence of Brahms's hearty taste for what we now call bonding. If he was a repressed homosexual, and there is no evidence to contradict this theory, we can be sure that he would have been as meticulous in his suppression of all evidence as he was in the destruction of any music he did not want the 'wide world' to hear.

More intriguing revelations about Brahms's feelings can be found in his letter of congratulations to Joachim, in February 1863, written on the occasion of Joachim's announcement of his engagement to Amalie Schneeweiss (which simply means 'snow-white'). The whole letter exhibits a mood that was both carefree and troubled; it is revealing in its charming straightforwardness. Here it is in full:

*'You lucky fellow! What more can I write, unless I add a few
more exclamations of the same kind! My wishes would sound
almost too solemn if I were to write them down.*

*No one will feel with you in your happiness as I do, more
particularly as your letter came upon me when I was in a dark
mood.*

*The whole time I have been here [Vienna] I have not ceased to
wonder whether, since I must guard against dreams of another
kind, I had not better experience and enjoy everything with one
exception, or whether I should make sure of one thing, that is, go
home and let all the rest slide.*

*And then you turn up and pluck the ripest and most beautiful
apple in Paradise for yourself.*

*What better can I wish than that everything will turn out as
lovely and good as the fact is in itself lovely and good and
desirable. With the addition of the beautiful 'snow-white' heart
of the apple, and the fine young apple trees, and more apples, and
more apples, &c. in infinitum.*

*Such is my most sincere wish, and I shall look forward to the
time when I can come and see you and, as I have already done at
the house of many a faithless friend, bend over a cradle and forget
everything in the contemplation of the laughing baby face.*

*Remember me very kindly to your fiancée. The name sounds
like a fairy-tale, and at first I did not know whether you were
giving me your pet name for her, or her real name!*

DEATH OF HIS FATHER

In February 1872, his father died. It fell to Brahms to help the
remaining members of his family, which he did gladly. Hamburg
was now remote in his life, however, and with the death of his
father, Vienna finally claimed him. His dutiful reconciliation with
Hamburg had to wait until the autumn of 1878, when he conducted his *Symphony No.2* there.

Brahms became increasingly happily entrenched in the city.
In refusing an appointment at Düsseldorf a few years later, he
remarked how, in Vienna, a bachelor attracted little notice, while
elsewhere such a man was a figure of fun. After a while, he began
to hanker after a fixed post. Characteristically, however, he wrote
to Joachim of the way in which his name was being put about as
a possible director of the *Singverein* or Choral Society of the Vienna

Gesellschaft der Musikfreunde, while adding that he dreads a formal offer since he would then have to make a decision. When Brahms did eventually receive the invitation to direct this very large and prestigious choir, in the autumn of 1872, it was in part the result of a blunt letter that he himself had written to the indecisive appointments committee! He held the post for three years, eventually relinquishing it rather than battle his way through all the latest intrigues.

His desire for a fixed post also coincides with an increasing reluctance to travel so much – although this hardly shows in the itineraries. Europe was not, after all, a totally unwarlike place, and hostilities – recent or actual – did not always make travelling a smooth process. In Brahms's lifetime, Bismarck's Prussia had already been involved in three wars: against Denmark in 1864 (over Schleswig-Holstein, where there had been an armistice since the year of European revolutions in 1848); against the other German states and Austria, in 1866; and, of course, against France in 1870–71.

UNLEASHING THE ORCHESTRA

Just as the death of his mother was followed by his completion of the *Requiem*, so the death of his father was followed by Brahms's determination at last to issue a symphony and so perpetuate the great tradition that had foundered after the death of Beethoven. It was a commonly-held view in the musical world at the time, and particularly in Vienna, that shoulders wide enough to carry the mantle of Beethoven had yet to be found.

Brahms had had relatively little hesitation in launching his career as composer with no fewer than three piano sonatas, all replete with references to Beethoven. Yet as a symphonist – not to say also, as a wiser man – Brahms was a little nervous of the comparison, and this was not helped by the fact that so much was by now expected of him. He had left it too late to produce an apprentice work, so Brahms made sure he was ready. After the first performances, Eduard Hanslick, slick as ever and right on cue, coined the notion in his review that Brahms's *First* was Beethoven's 'Tenth' – an unhelpful idea, as catchy as it is crass. Brahms was always going to write his first symphony when he was ready, on his own terms.

Brahms had tended, naturally enough, to work on music for

the forces he found himself amidst at the time, beginning with solo piano music written for himself to play, then piano-led chamber music, violin sonatas for his violinist friends, later the serenades for small orchestra when at Detmold, songs when a singer or text took his fancy, choral pieces once he had his Hamburg choir – and so on. Now with the *Requiem* behind him and the finest Viennese forces at his disposal, he could write anything. Portentous in its opening insistence, button-holing us until nearly throttled, then bursting then into savage exuberance, Brahms's *Symphony No.1 in C minor*, was first heard in Vienna, played by the Philharmonic, on 17 December 1876.

Its first performance had actually been given six weeks earlier, at Karlsruhe. Brahms had wanted to be sure that Vienna heard the work only after he had heard it himself. The atmosphere in Vienna was heightened by the fact that by then Brahms had relinquished his post, having given his last concert in April 1875. Just as the symphony's defiant opening signified Brahms's attitude to the tradition he was now at last continuing, so did the symphony's exuberance give a hint of the composer's sheer gratitude for three seasons' association with one of the greatest orchestras in the world.

It was at this point that von Bülow's careful admiration of Brahms broke out into utter enthusiasm. But Bülow's tendency to inflated silliness must not be allowed to detract from his honesty, nor from the dedicated manner in which he championed Brahms's work so greatly from that point on. Later, he was even instrumental in winning for Brahms the 'freedom of the city' of Hamburg, in 1889, a rare honour indeed, that he shared with Bismarck.

ROUTINE AND RECOGNITION

The momentum of the *First Symphony* quickly led to the *Second*, this time given its first performance in Vienna itself, under Hans Richter, on 30 December 1877. And that, in turn, led to the *Violin Concerto*, written for Joachim and given exactly a year later, on 1 January 1879, in Leipzig, with Joachim the soloist and Brahms conducting. Both these pieces were substantially written in Pörtschach, Carinthia, during his summer stay there. Brahms's established and well-paced routine now led to a good progression of steady composition, especially rich in songs. It was in Pörtschach in 1878 that he wrote the motet for unaccompanied choir, *'Warum ist das Licht gegeben?'* ('Wherefore is light given?' Op.74 No.1). A setting of Luther's translation of Job, it was a masterpiece of counterpoint intertwined with passionate emotions and yet also a searching, yearning expression of world-weariness finally resolved in sleep.

International recognition was secure by the late 1870s. Brahms attracted a special following in England, as Mendelssohn had done and Dvořák was to do, not least for their great choral works. The English composers Parry and Stamford, for example, were notable Brahmsians; the albeit stalwart sensitivity of their secular and 'Brahmsian' music is underestimated nowadays, perhaps through their association instead with a large succession of hymns still popular in the canon.

And more international recognition came in the form of honorary university degrees. The first was from Cambridge, in 1876/77, but Brahms, happy and honoured to accept, was daunted by the prospect of crossing the Channel. Wagner had nearly lost his life while crossing the North Sea and this gave him his inspiration for the storm in *The Flying Dutchman*; perhaps Brahms had that in mind? – at any rate, his terror got the better of him and he did not go, either at this or any other time. An ancient stipulation that recipients of honorary Cambridge degrees must attend in person stood in the way of him receiving the award, and Brahms tried to appease the university by sending Joachim across instead, equipped with no less than the manuscript of the *First Symphony*. It says much for Brahms's interest in such an award that he sent such a prize bribe and it says more about Cambridge's indelible sense of tradition and etiquette that it kept the manuscript but gave no degree.

Two years later, the university at Breslau also offered Brahms an honorary doctorate, which he accepted by post. This was not sufficient either, and he was cajoled shortly afterwards, in 1880, into writing the *'Academic Festival' Overture* in recognition of the honour. This overture was also the first product of a new summer venue for his working holidays, at Ischl, a royal spa not far from Salzburg, to which he returned again and again.

His first trip to Italy did not happen until 1878, and whereas he had never greatly cared for the French, his attitude to the Italians was markedly different; in the biographer Niemann's words, 'he simply refused to see the many dark blots on the radiant escutcheon of that glorious land and its highly talented people.' Quite. For Brahms, Italy meant escape. It was in Italy that he grew his beard ('a clean-shaven man,' he explained, 'is taken for an actor or a priest!') and where – eventually – he first made a journey by ship, crossing to Sicily. He enjoyed not so much the music of Italy but the art, the walks – and the wine.

CHAPTER 7

BRAHMS TURNS FIFTY
(1880–90)

- ♦ *Quarrels and reconciliations*
- ♦ *The last orchestral works*
- ♦ *Return to chamber music*

The first hint of autumn in his life came in the early 1880s, as Brahms approached fifty. Cracks appear in the happy pattern of his life and inspiration. First he had a quarrel with Joachim of all people, then, in 1882, came the death of Nottebohm, a great friend – the first of a sequence of losses that cast a shadow over the composer's life.

The quarrel with Joachim has something of the flavour of the manifesto fiasco in which they both participated all those years before. Brahms wrote a text he would regret.

The scenario was that Joachim, by nature a jealous man, had always had strained relations with his wife, Amalie, and it often fell to Brahms to act as intermediary. Brahms had always tended to think Joachim's behaviour the less reasoned or reasonable. On this occasion he said so to Amalie, in a letter all too blunt about Joachim's faults and adamant as to Amalie's innocence of any charge of infidelity. (Both men had quite realistic appraisals of each other, after all.) In private this letter might only have done good, but Amalie used it in court when Joachim eventually sued for divorce. He lost his case and for a while broke off his relationship with Brahms.

It was not exactly Brahms's fault, although he had given Amalie permission to use the letter when perhaps he should first have thought about other ways of establishing her innocence in court without alienating his old friend. Perhaps again it never occurred to him that harm could be done. That he should have lost his friend in the throes of a couple's battle adds spice to the manner in which he ultimately contrived to repair the damage, six years later – by writing a new concerto, not for Joachim alone but for *two* instruments – for violin and cello. The argumentative and gruffly devoted unison of the '*Double*' *Concerto* makes for one of the deepest expressions of bad-tempered love in any art before Picasso.

A similar blunder occurred between Brahms and Hans von Bülow. The old friend had had the historically unenviable lot of being in sympathy with all the various musical factions, the Lisztians, the Wagnerians, the Brahmsians and so on; he had also married Liszt's daughter Cosima, only to lose her to Wagner. In 1880, he accepted an appointment at the court of the Duke of Saxe-Meiningen, which gave him a good orchestra of modest proportions with which Brahms gave the first performance of the *Symphony No. 4* in 1885. This was agreed between them; it was also agreed that Brahms should take the orchestra on tour with the symphony, but Bülow was mortified to find the composer presenting the work in Frankfurt a few days ahead of plan, where it had been scheduled that Bülow should give it first. He was deeply insulted by this and imagined he had been humiliated. Brahms, in his exuberance, had quite overlooked the possibility of giving offence and it required a short period of time to elapse and a gentle gesture from the composer to restore things fully between them. He did so by sending Bülow his card, simply inscribed with a quotation from Mozart's *The Magic Flute* – 'Shall I see thee never again?' He quickly did.

It says much of the practical success of Brahms's routine that the story of his life could have reached 1887, the year of the *Double Concerto*, and Brahms in his fifty-fifth year, with little more incident than such as this. Of course, in the meantime, since 1880, he went on to complete a second *Piano Concerto* and the *Third* and *Fourth Symphonies*. His output continued just as he wished – just as he took his holidays as he wished and with whom he wished. He had celebrated his fiftieth birthday as he had wished – a bachelor supper with Billroth, Hanslick and one Arthur Faber.

Yet his music was changing all the time. The music around him was becoming bigger and bigger – we have only to think of the huge symphonies that Bruckner was writing, as an example. That the last of Brahms's symphonies should have been written with rather a small orchestra in mind is of significance; and, equally so, that the last concerto he was to write should be for two instruments, not one, according to baroque practice rather than to the gargantuan showpieces of the second half of the century. He had been editing Schubert's symphonies in 1884/85, it is true, which would have reminded him in depth of a lighter touch in symphonic writing – but the significance runs deeper than that.

Both the *Symphony No.4* and the '*Double*' *Concerto* point to a fusion of scale that is the hallmark of Brahms's greatest achievement, not only here but equally in the small late piano pieces that were yet to come. It is as if the confusions of symphonies and concertos and chamber scale of his earlier essays have all been resolved in a new way. The tendency to play Brahms with too large an orchestra is a loss in these works in particular. My recent recollection of a performance in Edinburgh of the '*Double*' *Concerto*, given by a local professional orchestra of modest proportions much as Tovey himself would have had at his disposal, was that the chamber music atmosphere between all the players was a revelation.

The short piano pieces that Brahms went on to write were to have an influence upon the mercurial scale of the young Debussy's subsequent piano music, and it is intriguing for the way both composers seem to go into the sound of the piano like an explorer peeling back layers of undergrowth. The lingering fascination with the musical qualities that are able to be contained in a few notes made for a deep sympathy between the two minds. (The old story that Debussy contrived a meeting with Brahms in Vienna in 1887 is nowadays discredited.) Although Debussy's pieces always have naturalistic, impressionistic titles, he was inclined to have these titles printed at the end of the piece, not as the title – as if to say: 'The music comes first.' Like Brahms, Debussy was also interested in making something poetic from specific technical challenges to the player's keyboard ability.

As for titles, something of Brahms's character can be gleaned from the carefully 'dated' or even archaic titles he gave to his pieces, especially these later piano works, where words such as '*Intermezzo*' and '*Capriccio*' occur. Their slightly antique character neatly conceals the extent of their innovation and sheer musical resourcefulness.

Brahms's large orchestral works in this decade stand amidst the renewed and rich output of chamber music – sonatas, trios and quintets – all culminating in the large chamber work that, in his vague way, he intended as his last – the *String Quartet No.3*. This was first heard in 1890. Indeed, all of the chamber music from Brahms's last years is as 'big' as the list is long: after the *Piano Trio No.2*, Op.87 of 1880/82 and the *String Quintet No.1*, Op.88 of 1882, there came, between 1887 and 1891: *Cello Sonata No.2*, Op.99; *Violin Sonata No.2*, Op.100; *Piano Trio No.3*, Op.101; *Violin Sonata No.3*, Op.108; *String Quintet No.2*, Op.111; and to top it all, an exceptional (and substantial) revision of an earlier work, the *Piano Trio*, Op.8.

With that, Brahms planned to retire, after a splendid festival in his honour, hosted in Hamburg in 1889. He drafted his will with the gently morbid air of routine that he had found so congenial in the Viennese attitude to life, while jesting with his friends that there was no need for it – that he was in fantastically good health. True, he drafted it; equally true, it was still only in draft form when he died six or seven years later.

CHAPTER 8
THE CLARINET YEARS
(1891–97)

- ♦ Brahms hears the clarinettist Richard Mühlfeld
- ♦ Renewed inspiration for chamber music
- ♦ Deaths of many friends
- ♦ Death of Clara Schumann
- ♦ Final illness and death

His sixtieth year approached in ambling peace and contentment, but Brahms was to be taken by surprise – by sound itself, by the sound of the clarinet, heard at Meiningen in 1891. This had an effect on him like that of the cor anglais upon Tristan in the third act of Wagner's drama: he 'heard light'.

The player was Richard Mühlfeld (1856–1907) and by a combination of his fine playing and the special quality of his actual instrument, he gave Brahms a renewed need to compose. The encounter with Mühlfeld resulted in no fewer than four great works: a quintet and trio, written first, in 1891, followed in 1894 by two sonatas. Between them came the substantial task of finishing the small piano pieces.

Mühlfeld was self-taught on the clarinet, having started as a violinist, and apart from being first clarinet of the orchestra at Meiningen he was also, from 1884 to 1896, first clarinet at Wagner's Bayreuth Festival. Clarinettists have more than one instrument, to cope with different key signatures, and of these his B flat and A clarinets have survived, but not the C clarinet. They were made by Ottensteiner of Münich in the mid-1870s, with a system of keys that uses fewer tone-holes in the instrument than other systems either then or now, giving an attractively gentle resonance. They are pitched at what then was an old-fashionedly low pitch (around a'=440) and Clara Schumann would have her piano tuned down to play with Mühlfeld.

It is all too easy to label these works 'reflective and autumnal' – and correct, what is more – yet it is less easy to be precise as to just what it is they reflect on. The reflective aspect, it cannot be denied, is autumnal enough seen in the context of a man who has found his friends tending to die off, even though he himself is only just turning sixty.

Marxsen had died in 1887, his sister and an old friend, Elizabeth von Herzogenberg, died in 1892, Billroth, von Bülow and Spitta, the great biographer of Bach's life and one of Brahms's favourite scholar friends, all died in 1894, and Clara in 1896. Indeed, he spent his sixtieth birthday keeping company with his walking companion Widmann, who was in bed with a broken foot. This gives a reflective but rather happy image of just the uncomplicated type of friendship that Brahms treasured above all. He had known the Swiss poet and pastor Victor Widmann since a summer holiday back in 1874, and Widmann later wrote a fond and frank account of their long friendship.

Joachim outlived Brahms, but, as he wrote to a friend after Brahms's death, 'We still have his works – as an individual I counted for little with him during the last years of his life.' There is no way that Brahms had it in his character to rage against death in the manner of Beethoven, and yet, in that same letter, Joachim had also said, 'I suffered much beforehand in seeing him gradually lose his hold on life; we must be thankful that his sufferings were not prolonged. The almost superhuman energy with which he resisted death was amazing!'

But Joachim was thinking of how Brahms persisted to the very last in his routine, in concert-going and visits, in concealing his decline – quite the opposite of the spectacular fist raised against the Almighty that is heard in the last movement of Beethoven's *Missa Solemnis*.

His taste for melancholy, however energetically that melancholy was expressed at times, does inform the wisdom of these last works, but it does nothing to highlight or explain their curiosity, their haunting sense of still inquiry. Indeed, despite their patently autumnal colours, it is possible to hear the beginnings of a sort of clarity that made the tweedy music critic and cricket-lover Sir Neville Cardus write:

The supremely beautiful Intermezzo, in E flat minor, *of Op.118, in which Brahms poured out his sorrow at the death of Elizabeth von Herzogenberg, has a truly great tragic intensity and disturbance. When we consider, too, Opp.118 and 119 of Brahms it is possible to think there was a vein of music in him still to be opened: he died maybe, only in his 'second' period, and wastefully was not permitted to live to see the world and music with that simple clarification of vision which came to Beethoven in the end.*

In his early piano works, the sonatas especially, he rides the music like a horse; in the later works he smooths and brushes it, close to its texture and heartbeat. The sheer fascination is so riveting that we realize that it has something to do with a fascination at life itself. His creative energies were renewed by music, by Mühlfeld and his clarinet, and that in itself provided an extreme pretext for curiosity. Perhaps he was reminded of the way in which even in the extremes of his madness, it was music that drew from Schumann sense and coherent energy.

It is this mood that then gives rise to his four last songs, entitled with an almost morbidly ironic grandiloquence '*Vier ernste Gesänge*' ('Four Serious Songs'). To texts mainly from Ecclesiastes, they are concerned not with the final religious quandary of an atheist but with a last statement of the power of Love to hold everything together. It is Love, after all, that holds the whole of Brahms's output together. The set is not a cycle of songs, as in the narrative cycles written by Schubert, but its progression from the darkest tones of the bitterness of inevitable death to the point at which 'the greatest of these is Love' – the last words Brahms set – makes for an extraordinary unity across four 'movements'.

Cardus was unusual for seeing in the late works the possibility that Brahms was onto something new. He was not alone, however, in suggesting a parallel between the poet Thomas Hardy – born in 1840 – and Brahms; both shared a sturdy quality of spirituality and religious unbelief, as well as a devotion to landscape as the deepest metaphor for the human condition. Equally, in the words of one of Hardy's finest moments, as we know from the range of pictures conjured by Brahms's songs, Brahms was a man 'who used to notice such things'.

All the same, it is important to see that where Hardy's outlook was one of acidic pessimism, Brahms's was not. For Hardy, as for Nietzsche before him, the 'death of God' was the cause of great despair, rage or even glee; for Brahms, another cigar and a coffee, please – he had read of the death in yesterday's paper.

An aspect of these final years was Brahms's relationship to the new music around him. He was at the heart of it, if only by virtue of being at the heart of Vienna. And at the heart of the factions now, too. He was every bit as grumpy in his taste as we might expect, not caring at all for the supposedly Wagnerian Bruckner (1824–96), nor for Hugo Wolf (1860–1903).

Wolf was a special case, not least for becoming, in the 1890s, the only serious rival to Brahms as a songwriter. Like Richard Strauss (1864–1947), Wolf had actually presented early work to Brahms, who had advised him to study counterpoint; it was advice ill-suited to Wolf's undisciplined way of composing, and the highly-strung Wolf had thereafter attacked Brahms's conservatism in the press. Strauss's inclination to give a poetic programme to the *Symphony No.4*, a storyline for each movement, was far too reminiscent of Liszt – and thus of Wagner too – for Brahms's taste.

Not all composers left Brahms feeling disgruntled. In 1896, Edvard Grieg visited him, and Brahms sat beside Dvořák for the Vienna premiere of his *Ninth Symphony*, the so-called '*New World*'. (Like Brahms, by the way, Dvořák also came to have a reputation for wearing his old clothes about the place.) By then, he had also met Mahler (1860–1911), whose music dismayed him but whose conducting he regarded as uniquely fine. We should not be too harsh on Brahms's judgment of Mahler, and it is easy to understand how he was unhappy to look forward into the future with the same exploratory relish with which he ransacked the past.

It was also in 1896, in what was to be his last year, that Brahms tidied his life, destroying what sketches and such things had survived his usually ruthless methods. It was also in 1896 that Clara Schumann died, in Frankfurt, on 20 May, after fluctuating health following a stroke in March. Brahms, on holiday after false hopes of her recovery, had to make the journey by train to her funeral service, in several stages, and managed to miss a connection, which gave him an even worse journey. He arrived too late, indeed, and was forced to follow immediately to Bonn, where

Clara was to be buried beside Schumann himself. He returned not to Vienna but to Ischl, where he had been holidaying, but he was not well and in July went to see a doctor – which, for Brahms, was quite a concession. He was not told how serious his condition was, but by the time he reached Vienna again in the October, there was no remaining doubt that he was suffering from cancer of the liver. He was still not told the prognosis, but, as happens so often with cancer patients, the silent tact of doctors and friends seems to have been matched by an inner knowledge already in place.

Weakening even through bouts of optimistic better health, Brahms continued to go to concerts and to the opera, even into the New Year of 1897; he heard the Joachim Quartet play twice in early January. The last visit to the theatre was to see an operetta by Johann Strauss II (his last), but he could not keep his strength up and had to go home early. When he was too frail to take his walks, friends provided their carriages. Only a fortnight before his death he heard his last concert, given at the Wittgenstein house by Mühlfeld and friends who, on realizing the composer's exhaustion, asked him which of the two works they were to play he would prefer to hear, his own *Clarinet Quintet* or Weber's. He chose the Weber.

It is curious to reflect that in that very room the children of the Wittgenstein family would have been present: Paul, later to be a distinguished pianist and, after losing his right arm, the champion of the left-hand repertoire (he commissioned the Ravel *Concerto*), and Ludwig, the philosopher, who later remarked so succinctly in a notebook on the centenary of composer's birth: 'In Brahms, the overwhelming sense of "I can". . .'

Three weeks after that concert, that power ran out, and Brahms died peacefully, in his home, on the morning of 3 April, 1897. The funeral procession to Vienna's *Zentralfriedhof* was the most extravagant since Beethoven's. He was buried alongside Beethoven and Schubert.

CHAPTER 9
BRAHMS ON RECORD

For the purpose of discussing recordings of his work, Brahms's output has been organized according to type. Catalogue numbers have not been given, at least partly because discs have all manner of different numbers in different countries. Some recordings come in and out of circulation at an alarming speed, what's more – each time with new numbers. Any serious music-lover should not be too proud to consider second-hand compact discs, nor too devoted to technology to disdain second-hand long-playing records. In any case, no decent shop will refuse to locate a record referred to by the name of the piece and the name(s) of the performer(s). I have given dates of recordings and details of record companies in general only if confusion is likely to arise.

It will become clear that I personally place musical values above those of impressive sound quality; even to the extent of preferring 'live' performances, complete with performers' slips and audience noise, to the cleanliness achieved so impressively in the recording studio – the technical cleanliness of an operating theatre perhaps, but achieved as often as not only by means of emotional anaesthetic. Brahms himself became splashy and temperamental as a player; I see no need to break the tradition.

THE TRADITION

The tradition was started by Brahms himself, on a single crackle-rich Edison cylinder. Nonetheless, the early days of rather more audible recording have given us many 'sides' by players who knew Brahms – violinists especially. Joachim himself made five records, in 1903, two of music by Brahms; the reissue by Pearl/Opal is a marvellous glimpse back into the nineteenth century. So, too, a *Hungarian Dance* recorded by Leopold Auer (1845–1930) with gusto and pluck, recorded just after World War One and reissued on Appian. Early violinists always seemed duty-bound to record at least one *Hungarian Dance*! As for pianists, the catalogue is best served again by Pearl and Appian, Pearl having issued sets of records by 'The Pupils of Liszt' and 'The Pupils of Clara Schumann'; the latter set (of 6 discs) includes the Edison cylinder recording by Brahms.

Composers influenced by Brahms included such diverse figures as Eugen d'Albert – a pianist who played Brahms's concertos in the composer's last concerts – as well as the English Brahmsians Charles Villiers Stanford and Hubert Parry; almost the only company to have done anything about investigating the fascinating and rewarding Romantic repertoire off the beaten track of the warhorse masterpieces is Hyperion; their list includes a *Piano Trio* by Clara Schumann as well.

THE TWO STYLES

Brahms was a divided character: the solidity of his music is not block-like, but a sure balance of extremes – a balance between love and reticence, passion and control, speed and rest, the energy to be moving on and a tender wistfulness for what has been and for what might have been. The same is true of the styles in which his music is played. Brahms knew both extremes – they inhabit his music as they did his life, and the performer must be alert to both.

Equally, performers tend to come down on one side or the other. So, in the symphonies to begin with, we have the contrast of Furtwängler, luxuriant and wayward, and Toscanini, strict and taut. There is a traditional rivalry between the supporters of both these conductors, and in Brahms, their conflicting characteristics are more evident than in any other music, even Beethoven's. Both are tremendous, not least because both are sure of what they are doing. Alongside them, other conductors seem half-hearted or merely vulgar, indulging in big sound or the big gesture. When Furtwängler wrote that 'Brahms's greatness lies in his strictness. Each of his works, whether large or small, sweet or tragic, is bound together as if with iron bonds,' he pinpoints the essence of *both* styles.

TOSCANINI AND FURTWÄNGLER

Two versions of the symphonies have come to us by Toscanini, one set (on RCA) with the NBC Symphony Orchestra and another, less easily found, taken from concerts he gave in the hardly completed Royal Festival Hall in London, in 1952, with the Philharmonia Orchestra. The latter is preferable, but seldom issued in such good sound as the studio recordings. There is also an athletic *Piano Concerto No.2* with Vladimir Horowitz, and a rumbustious account of the '*Double' Concerto* (also on video).

A number of different performances by Wilhelm Furtwängler survive. They are not all the same as each other. All are unexpected and gripping. Most extraordinary are a *Symphony No.1* with the North-West German Radio Symphony Orchestra (Hamburg, 27 October 1951) and a *Symphony No.4* with the Berlin Philharmonic Orchestra (Wiesbaden, June 1949); and the *Piano Concerto No.2* – twice, with Adrian Aeschbacher and the BPO (December 1943), more tempestuous and risky even than that with Edwin Fischer (BPO 1942). These three works catch Furtwängler at his best in Brahms.

With Yehudi Menuhin, he recorded the *Violin Concerto* twice, once with the Philharmonia and once with the Lucerne Festival Orchestra (1949), a lesser band that gives a greater performance nonetheless. A 'live' performance with Gioconda de Vito, given in Turin in 1952, has an exploratory quality present in few others.

THE 'GERMAN' REQUIEM

Furtwängler's performance of the *Requiem* in Stockholm in 1948 gives some idea of the piece at its limit. The problem with most other conductors is that the balance between reverence and sheer ponderous speeds is a failure. Despite the fact that, to my taste, Herbert von Karajan's Brahms is elsewhere slick and vain in an utterly unBrahmsian manner, his first recording of the *Requiem*, made in 1947 (on EMI, with the Philharmonia, Elisabeth Schwarzkopf and Hans Hotter), is mesmerizing.

Willem Mengelberg, Ernest Ansermet and Bruno Walter made interesting recordings of the piece. John Eliot Gardiner's version uses forces more on the smaller, 'authentic' scale and delivers an interestingly different texture without however quite the same impressively gothic commitment as Klemperer or Giulini.

THE SYMPHONIES

Names such as Otto Klemperer and Carlo Maria Giulini belong to the centre of the tradition of Brahms's symphonies. Along with

Karl Böhm (whose neglected Vienna Philharmonic set on DG from the mid-1970s I have long admired), these figures ply a course between the two extremes epitomized by Furtwängler and Toscanini. Klemperer is particularly at home in the *Symphony No.1*, and Giulini in *No.4*.

As far as other complete sets of all four symphonies go, in the stereo age I have heard nothing to compare with the ASV set by the Royal Liverpool Philharmonic under Marek Janowski. It has been issued on separate discs. Beside Janowski, other versions, Claudio Abbado's recent digital set, for example, seem bombastic and governed more by the requirements of hi-fi salesmen than by Brahms's subtlety. Janowski achieves a marvellously chamber exuberance in the strings' phrasing that is a constant delight, in the *Symphony No.4* especially. The playing is refreshingly self-ef-facing, and the only rival, at the other extreme of self-expression but of supreme power, is the set compiled by Leonard Bernstein (on DG, with all the concertos as well): for stereo and sonic fusspots these are performances to compensate for the monaural performances by Furtwängler.

One-off performances abound, especially of the *Symphony No.3*. By far the most characterful is a live performance by Sir Thomas Beecham with the NBCSO – he can be heard wailing and hollering encouragement – but it is not easy to track down. There are nearly as vibrant efforts from Mengelberg and Leopold Stokowski as well as a neat and crisp account from Serge Kousse-vitsky with the Boston Symphony Orchestra.

Of the other symphonies in one-off performances, Jasha Horenstein's version of the *No.2* (Danish Radio Symphony Or-chestra) and Victor DeSabata's of the *Fourth* (Berlin Philharmonic Orchestra) are special. A *Symphony No.1* conducted by the cellist Pablo Casals is unfortunately not as fine as his conducting of Beethoven or Mendelssohn. His early account of the '*Double*' *Concerto*, however, with Jacques Thibaud, is splendid and erratic.

THE CONCERTOS

There are fine versions of both *Piano Concertos* with pianists Rudolf Serkin, Claudio Arrau (especially the earlier set under Giulini on EMI), Emil Gilels and Maurizio Pollini, to put them in chronological order; too many versions are as if constipated or cramped by the idea of making a perfect recording of a big piece, and imagination seems to come low on the list of priorities.

Performances of the *Piano Concerto No.1* need to understand bluff in its first movement. Of the older generation Schnabel has it, with Szell, and in the stereo age Woodward too (on RCA), with Masur, in many ways the most satisfying performance of all. A chamber music mood is established in the first movement by Gary Graffman with Münch, but the last movements are not on quite so high a level of imagination. The finest account of this concerto I have heard in concert was with Dmitri Alexeev, whose Brahms recordings are exceptional.

In an account of the *Piano Concerto No.2* given by Gerhard Oppitz with the ever under-rated and usually marvellous Sir Colin Davis conducting the Bavarian Radio Orchestra (on RCA), the revelation of chamber-like orchestral texture is a thrilling surprise at least as fine as Oppitz's playing. A rickety old recording of Elly Ney demands affection, and the Aeshbacher with Furt-wängler demands a seat-belt.

The *Violin Concerto* has brought out the best in many players; Yehudi Menuhin, of course, but also Joseph Szigeti – with Ham-ilton Harty, a scintillating recording from 1929 – Fritz Kreisler, Ginettè Neveu, Nathan Milstein (with Eugen Jochum) and others; I have always loved an old Columbia record made by Johanna Martzy with the Philharmonia under Paul Kletzki. There is a bizarre but useful recording by Ruggiero Ricci (on Biddulph) in which, capitalizing on CD technology, he offers no fewer than seventeen cadenzas for the first movement, from which you can select at will.

As for the '*Double*' *Concerto*, everyone does well but there always seems to come a point at which it does not quite work. Furtwängler and Toscanini both accompany arresting versions, but my favourites have long been that with Josef Suk and André Navarro the soloists and the Czech Philharmonic conducted by Karel Ancerl in the early 1960s (Supraphon) or Alfredo Campoli and Navarro again, with the Hallé under Barbirolli (Pye).

CHAMBER MUSIC WITHOUT PIANO

The string sextets and quintets have been collected in a set focused around the Amadeus Quartet and it is a fine feast of Brahms. There are few better performances that do not involve Pablo Casals, but those that do are cooked to an even greater perfection.

The *Clarinet Quintet* was recorded in 1928 by Charles Draper, a friend of Mühlfeld's, with the Léner Quartet; its reissue on Pearl (with the Mozart) is a treasure, not at all indulgent but overwhelmingly true. Still, I like a certain roughness in this piece and have fond memories of performances by the Allegri Quartet and by the Edinburgh Quartet, the latter being available on cassette. Reginald Kell and the Busch Quartet is still a vision apart. For a smoother reading, there is an enduring version by members of the Vienna Octet (Decca).

For the *String Quartets* there is a mixture of recommendations to be made. As with Beethoven, the Busch Quartet gives a special way of playing that is wide-eyed in wonder and power. One day the old records by the Végh Quartet will be easily available, and easily the best, the laziness and the detail are so perfectly knowing, so perfectly Brahmsian. Their nearest rivals meantime are the Janáček Quartet on Supraphon and the Lindsays on ASV.

CHAMBER MUSIC WITH PIANO

The obvious starting point is the *Piano Quintet*, which has been through dozens of recordings. How to choose? The domestic and amiable quality should be a special thrill to us, but the piece is often a vehicle of heavy would-be symphonic emphasis. There is, however, an old recording made by Eva Bernáthová and the Janáček Quartet in about 1960, where one feels almost embarrassed to have blundered into the music room of a close friend. Otherwise, versions with pianists Rudolf Serkin (with the Busch Quartet), Leon Fleischer (with the Juilliard Quartet – my next favourite after the one with Bernáthová), Sviatoslav Richter (with the Borodin Quartet) and Pollini (with the Quartetto Italiano) stand out.

Fright at the trotting tempo with which Glenn Gould and the Toronto String Quartet despatch the *andante* second movement of the *Piano Quintet* turns to a wry smile at the thought that Gould may have had in mind Brahms's reputation for walking exhaustingly fast on his country hikes. It is a challenging interpretation.

The *Piano Quartets* have fared less well. There are three: the pair that make Opps.25 and 26, and then the all but tragic work that stands not only emotionally at the heart of Brahms's output but arithmetically in the middle too – the *Piano Quartet in C minor*,

Op.60. The first two have been recorded rather more often than the third. Although there are fine sets of all three with Artur Rubinstein and the Guarneri Quartet (lean and loving), and Victor Aller and the Hollywood Quartet (lean and exact), the CBS set with Emanuel Ax, Isaac Stern, Jaime Laredo and Yo-Yo Ma has the greatest sense of occasion, the Op.60 especially satisfactory, with its train-like energies and Hamlet-like dilemmas.

Rudolf Serkin and the Busch String Quartet recorded the Opp.25 and 26 in versions that, despite various lapses, remain the most entranced and entrancing. Recordings of one or other of those two, with pianists Edwin Fischer, Emil Gilels, Sviatoslav Richter or Christoph Eschenbach, are all substantial.

The *Piano Trios* have done much better. It is clear that players feel much happier here – and perhaps less challenged. I used always to adore above all others the versions on CBS by Stern-Rose-Istomin, but a more recent issue on Chandos, by the Bekova Sisters, gives them a very close run. Any recording involving Pablo Casals, of any of these pieces (or indeed of the *Cello Sonatas*), promises wild glimpses of passionate insight, while a thrilling recording by Myra Hess, Jelly d'Arányi and Gaspar Cassadó of the *Piano Trio No.3*, Op.87 (made in 1935 and reissued by Appian in a set devoted to Myra Hess) yields up the grotesque in the *presto* third movement in an astonishingly vivid, unique manner.

Amongst other older records is also a gruff but excitedly lyrical performance of the *Clarinet Trio*, with the clarinettist Charles Draper, the cellist W.H. Squire, and Hamilton Harty at the piano, records made in 1925 but as far as I know, yet to be reissued. Their day will come.

INSTRUMENTAL SONATAS

The way in which cellists yearn their lives into the Brahms *Cello Sonatas* is moving enough in itself and brings the best from them. The following recordings are utterly winning: William Conway (with Peter Evans), Michaela Fukacová (with Iván Klánsky), János Starker (and – at least three different pianists over the years); so too is a sprightly record by Rostropovich and Serkin. It goes without saying that Casals lets himself go and takes you with him; Jacqueline du Pré also.

The *Violin Sonatas* are in general less successfully done. Appian have put out a fascinating disc of Adolf Busch and Serkin in the first two sonatas (and Schumann's *First*) which should not be overlooked. For complete sets of all three sonatas, however, there are Igor Oistrakh (with Natalia Zertsalova), Josef Suk (with Julius Katchen) and two sets by Itzhak Perlman (with Vladimir Ashkenazy or Daniel Barenboim). Of the most recent records, Gidon Kremer is most impressive, with Martha Argerich.

With the *Viola Sonatas* and *Clarinet Sonatas* the choice is thin enough for you to take what comes. Note that Keith Puddy has made a record of the *Clarinet Sonatas* on Mühlfeld's own instrument, accompanied by Malcolm Martineau on a contemporary Bechstein piano, and very satisfying it is too.

PIANO MUSIC

The complete set of solo piano music by Julius Katchen, issued by Decca in the mid-1960s, has an enduring, inexhaustible wonder about it: just when you want Brahms more Romantic or just when you want him more strictly Classical than before, it is there already in Katchen's loving and insightful playing. This judicious yet spontaneous playing is unrivalled, though a peculiarly bright complete set, rather Viennese in character, by Walter Klien (Vox) should not be dismissed – if you can find it.

Katchen also recorded the *Violin Sonatas* and the *Piano Trios* with Josef Suk and János Starker; their glories are revealed more on repeated hearing than right away.

Other pianists have recorded less than the complete works. Of these, Claudio Arrau, Krystian Zimerman, Stephen (Bishop-) Kovacevich and Sviatoslav Richter stand out. The first two have made stunning records of the early works (sonatas and/or variations), the latter two of the later works. Rudolf Serkin recorded too little Brahms, but what there is (some of the variations especially) is gritty and gripping. Schnabel recorded only the two *Rhapsodies* Op.79, but nobody plays them better. Arturo Benedetti Michelangeli's set of the *Ballades*, Op.10, is a revelation, looking forward to Debussy; Glenn Gould's is also a revelation, looking backwards to Bach.

The sonatas pose special problems, since the texture is often surprisingly thin; there are few notes and at the keyboard, pianists must not be afraid to fortify the sound by sheer fist when required. It is the prime example of his style as a young touring virtuoso performer. Zimerman's performances in concert, for example, have a weight of muscle he has never allowed himself in the studio. Richter's recordings of the sonatas are fine as well, and there is a grand reading of Op.5 by Edwin Fischer on EMI Références, coupled with his exceptional Schumann *Fantasy* Op.17.

On the subject of Schumann, Claudio Arrau, Maurizio Pollini, Charles Rosen and Dino Ciani have all made exciting records of both the *Fantasy* and the *Sonata in F sharp minor*, Op.11. Pearl has issued a set tracing the recordings of 'Pupils of Clara Schumann', giving insight into that tradition, and similar treasures are to be found in the Appian catalogue. ASV has issued a fascinating disc by Stephen Mayer, which celebrates the 1837 Thalberg–Liszt duel.

SONGS

A problem with recommendations here is that so many items are to be found on anthologies of music not all by Brahms. For instance, an old record by Mattiwilda Dobbs with Gerald Moore has only four Brahms songs, but each is a gem. Historical anthologies from Acanta and (coupled with Schumann) from EMI each provide a happy way of collecting different singers without too much overlap of material.

Some of the absolutely finest Brahms singing can be had from Tiana Lemnitz, Elisabeth Schumann, Christa Ludwig (especially an astonishing 'live' recital with Leonard Bernstein at the piano), Margaret Price, Leo Slezak, Hermann Prey, Hans Hotter, and Alexander Kipnis; there is even a bewildering recital by Kirsten Flagstad, full of marvellous things, as well as similar surprises from Grace Bumbry in her all-too-rare ventures into song. Other singers not to be neglected are Elisabeth Schwarzkopf, mannered as she is, and Ernst Häfliger, unmannered as he is. Thomas Allen sings with a warm-smiled honesty that is engaging.

JOHANNES BRAHMS: COMPLETE LIST OF WORKS

Brahms tended only to publish his work after long deliberation and revision. Therefore the published order, especially as expressed by the opus numbering, while reflecting fairly accurately the chronological order of Brahms's satisfaction with his music, is rather less indicative of the order even of completion, let alone gestation.

In the list that follows, I have tried to present his work in an order that reflects the chronology of his creative output. Where only one date is given (in round brackets), it is simply the date of first publication, if that also best suggests the period of the work; where a second date is given, that is the date of first publication if significantly later than the period of composition.

LANGUAGE

In this list, designed not to be cumbersome to an English-speaking reader, works are given their title in German only if that form is at all commonly used in English; but translations are given where the two languages seem equally common in usage. The reader will see the way in which organization of such things can nonetheless become too literal, by noting with a smile that in spoken English the *Liebeslieder-walzer* tend to be given the hybrid title, '*Liebeslieder* Waltzes'. The rendering 'Love-song Waltzes' may never have appeared in print before now.

THE COMPLETE EDITION

Brahms's complete works are published by Breitkopf & Härtel, in an edition of 26 volumes edited by Hans Gal and E. Mandyczewski (1926–28). Some volumes from this are reproduced by Dover Publications in soft covers.

OPUS NUMBERING

Like Beethoven's, the organization of Brahms's work has kept to his own opus numbers as published and has not been reorganized into numbers identified by an editor's name. Mozart has Köchel numbers, Schubert has Deutsch, and so on. As a mischievous piece of musical one-upmanship, I suggest the use of 'Bradshaw Numbers' for Brahms, in place of the unpoetic Opus numbers, after the name of the great Victorian international railway timetable and in acknowledgement of the way in which Brahms's pattern of working on different pieces at different times in different towns depended on a life spent travelling on the railways of Europe.

ARRANGEMENTS

Brahms had the habit of arranging his music for domestic forces such as piano duet, and these are recorded here alongside the original piece even where publication of the arrangement came a year or two later. Works in square brackets are the most significant works by other composers either edited by Brahms, or in his arrangements. The arrangements are for the original instrumentation unless otherwise stated.

CADENZAS

Brahms wrote cadenzas for five piano concertos:
- Bach, in D minor
- Mozart, in G, K.453 (two)
- Mozart, in D minor, K.466
- Mozart, in C minor, K.491
- Beethoven, in G, Op.58 (two)

All except the Beethoven (1907) were published first in 1927. Another cadenza for Mozart's K.466, edited by Paul Badura-Skoda (1980), is regarded as dubious.

VOLKSLIEDER : FOLKSONGS

Brahms made many collections of folksongs, some of which are to be found below in the ordinary listing. In addition, there were four sets of arrangements for four-part unaccompanied chorus, all published relatively recently:
- Seven Folksongs, arranged from Hamburg Women's Choir part-books (1940)
- Thirteen Folksongs, ed. Kross (1965)

◊ Twenty-six Folksongs, edd. Gotwals & Keppler (1968)
◊ Twenty-seven Folksongs, ed. Helms (1970)

EARLY AND ONE-OFF PIECES

◊ Under the pseudonym 'G.W. Marks': *Souvenir de la Russie*, Fantasias on Russian and Bohemian Airs, for piano (pre-1852)
◊ Hymn to the Veneration of the great Joachim: waltzes for two violins and bass or cello (1853 or before, 1976)
◊ From the Violin Sonata written for Joachim by Schumann and Dietrich: *Scherzo*, in C minor (1853, 1906)

THE 1850s

Op.4	*Scherzo*, in E flat minor, for piano (1851, 1854)
Op.2	Piano Sonata No.2, in F sharp minor (1852, 1854)
Op.1	Piano Sonata No.1, in C (1853)
Op.3	Six Songs (1853)
Op.6	Six Songs (1853)
~	*Die Müllerin* (incomplete song) (1853?, 1984)
Op.5	Piano Sonata No.3, in F minor (1854)
Op.7	Six Songs (1854)
Op.8	Piano Trio No.1, in B (1854) (revised version, 1891)
Op.9	Variations on a Theme by Schumann, for piano (1854)
[Arranged:	Schumann, *Scherzo* from Piano Quintet Op.44, for piano (1854)]
[Arranged:	Joachim, Overture to Shakespeare's *Henry IV*, Op.7, for two pianos (1855 or later, 1902)]
[Arranged:	Schumann, Piano Quartet, Op.47, for piano duet (1855, 1887)]
~	Two Gigues, for piano (1855, 1927)
~	Two Sarabandes, for piano (1855, 1917)
~	Two Gavottes, for piano (No.2 incomplete) (1854/55, 1979)
~	Fugue, in A flat, for organ (1856, 1864)
~	Two Preludes and Fugues, for organ (1856/57, 1927)
~	'Kyrie', for four-part mixed choir & continuo (1856, 1984)
~	Five Mass movements, for four- & six-part mixed choir (1856, 1984)

Op.10	Four Ballades, for piano (1856)
[Edited:	Schumann, Cantata for voices, choir & orchestra, Op.140 (1857)]
~	Fourteen *Volks-Kinderlieder*, for voice & piano (1858, 1926)
~	Twenty-eight *Deutsche Volkslieder* (1858, 1928)
~	Chorale Prelude and Fugue (*O Traurigkeit*), for organ (1858, 1882)
~	Piano Piece, in B flat (1859/62, 1979)
Op.15	Piano Concerto No.1, in D minor (1854/59, 1861) (also arranged for piano duet; and for two pianos)
Op.18	String Sextet No.1, in B flat (1859/60, 1862) (also arranged for piano duet)
~	Theme and Variations, in D minor, for piano (arrangement of slow movement of Op.18) (1860, 1927)

THE 1860s

Op.11	Serenade No.1, in D, for orchestra (1860) (also arranged for piano duet)
Op.16	Serenade No.2, in A, for small orchestra without violins (1860) (revised version, 1875) (also arranged for piano duet)
Op.12	'Ave Maria', for female voices, orchestra or organ (1861) (also arranged for piano with text)
Op.13	Funeral Hymn, for mixed voices & wind band (1861) (also arranged for piano with text)
Op.14	Eight Songs and Romances (1861)
Op.17	Four Partsongs, for female voices, two horns & harp (1861) (also arranged for piano with words)
Op.23	Variations on a Theme by Schumann, for piano duet (1861, 1863)
Op.19	Five Poems (Songs) (1862)
Op.20	Three Duets, for soprano & contralto (1862)
Op.21	Two Sets of Variations, for piano (1862): No.1, on an Original Theme No.2, on a Hungarian Theme (these possibly begun mid-1850s)

Op.22	*Marienlieder*, traditional songs for four-part mixed voices (1862)
Op.24	Variations and Fugue on a Theme by Handel, for piano (1862)
[Edited:	C.P.E. Bach, six Concertos for keyboard with string quartet (1862)]
Op.25	Piano Quartet No.1, in G minor (1863) (also arranged for piano duet)
Op.26	Piano Quartet No.2, in A (1863) (also arranged for piano duet)
Op.28	Four Duets, for contralto & baritone (1863)
~	Canon in F minor, for piano (1864, 1979)
Op.29	Two Motets, for five-part mixed voices (1864) (also arranged as rehearsal piano score)
Op.27	Psalm XIII, for female voices & organ (or piano) (1864)
Op.30	*Geistliches Lied*, for mixed voices & organ (or piano) (1864)
Op.31	Three Vocal Quartets, with piano (1864)
~	Fourteen *Deutsche Volkslieder*, for four-part chorus (1864) and:
~	Twelve Additional Songs (1864, 1927)
[Edited:	W.F. Bach, Sonata in F for two claviers (1864)]
[Edited:	Schubert, Twelve *Ländler*, Op.171 (1864)]
[Arranged:	C.P.E. Bach, two Violin Sonatas (1864)]
Op.32	Nine Songs (1865)
Op.33	Fifteen Romances from *Magelone* (text by Tieck): Set One, three songs (1865) Sets Two to Five, twelve songs (1869)
Op.36	String Sextet No.2, in G (1864/5, 1866) (also arranged for piano duet)
Op.34	Piano Quintet, in F minor (1865)
Op.34a	Sonata in F minor, for two pianos (earlier version of Op.34)
Op.37	Three Sacred Choruses, for female voices (1865)
Op.40	Horn Trio, in E flat (1865, 1866) (horn or cello or viola)
Op.35	Two Sets of Studies on a Theme by Paganini, for piano (1866)
Op.38	Cello Sonata No.1, in E minor (1866)

Op.39	Waltzes, for piano duet (1866) (also arranged for piano solo)
Op.44	Twelve Songs & Romances, for female voices (piano *ad lib.*) (1866)
[Edited:	Schumann, *Scherzo & Presto Passionato*, for piano (1866)]
Op.41	Five Partsongs, for male voices (1867)
Op.43	Four Songs (1868)
Op.46	Four Songs (1868)
Op.47	Five Songs (1868)
Op.48	Seven Songs (1868)
Op.49	Five Songs (1868)
[Edited:	Schubert, three *Impromptus* (1868/69)]
[Edited:	Schubert, Twenty *Ländler* for piano (1869) and: Twenty *Ländler* for piano duet (1869)]
Op.42	Three Partsongs, for six-part mixed voices (1869) (also arranged as rehearsal piano score)
Op.45	*Ein Deutsches Requiem* (A German Requiem), for soprano & baritone, chorus & orchestra (1860s/68, 1869) (also arranged for piano with words; and for piano duet without)
Op.50	*Rinaldo*, cantata with text from Goethe: for tenor, male chorus & orchestra (1869) (also arranged for piano with text)
~	Two Sets of Hungarian Dances, for piano duet (1869)
Op.52	*Liebeslieder-walzer*, for piano duet & voices *ad lib.* (1869)
[Arranged:	Chopin, *Étude*, in F minor, Op.25; and: Weber, final movement of Sonata, in C (1869)]

THE 1870s

Op.53	Rhapsody, for contralto, male chorus & orchestra (1870) (also arranged for piano with text)
[Edited:	Schubert, *Quartettsatz* in C minor (1870)]
[Arranged:	Handel, fifteen Continuo Realizations (1870)]
Op.54	*Schicksalslied* (Song of Destiny) (text by Hölderlin), for chorus & orchestra (1871) (also arranged for piano with text)

Op.57	Eight Daumer Songs (1871)
Op.58	Eight Songs (1871)
[Edited:	Couperin, Keyboard Pieces, books 1, 11 (1871)]
[Arranged:	Gluck, *Gavotte* (1871?)]
Op.55	*Triumphlied*, for chorus & orchestra (1872) (also arranged for piano with text; and for piano duet without)
~	*Regenlied*, for voice & piano (1872, 1908)

Op.51	Two String Quartets (1860s/70s, 1873):
	    No.1, in C minor
	    No.2, in A minor
	    (both also arranged for piano duet)

Op.59	Eight Songs (1873)
~	Five Ophelia Songs, from Shakespeare's *Hamlet* (1873, 1935)
Op.56a	Variations on a Theme by Haydn, for orchestra (1873, 1874)
Op.56b	Variations on a Theme by Haydn, for two pianos (1873)
[Edited:	Schumann, *Études Symphoniques*, Opp.13 & post. (1873)]
Op.52a	*Liebeslieder-walzer*, for vocal quartet & piano duet (1874)
~	Hungarian Dances Nos.1, 3, 10; arranged for orchestra (1874)
Op.61	Four Duets, for soprano & contralto (1874)
Op.62	Seven Partsongs, for mixed voices (1874)
Op.63	Nine Songs (1874)
Op.64	Three Vocal Quartets, with piano (1874)
Op.65	*Neue Liebeslieder-walzer*, for vocal quartet & piano duet (1875)
Op.65a	*Neue Liebeslieder-walzer*, for piano duet (arrangement of Op.65)
Op.60	Piano Quartet No.3, in C minor (1875)
Op.66	Five Duets, for soprano & contralto (1875)
Op.67	String Quartet No.3, in B flat (1876) (also arranged for piano duet)
Op.68	Symphony No.1, in C minor (1862/76, 1877) (also arranged for piano duet)
Op.69	Nine Songs (1877)

Op.70	Four Songs (1877)	
Op.71	Five Songs (1877)	
Op.72	Five Songs (1877)	
[Edited:	Mozart, *Requiem* (1877)]	
Op.73	Symphony No.2, in D (1877, 1878)	
	(also arranged for piano duet)	
Op.74	Two Motets, for mixed chorus (1878)	
Op.75	Four Ballads and Romances, for various vocal duets (1878)	
[Edited:	Chopin, Sonatas Nos.2 & 3, Opp.35 & 58 (1878)]	
[Arranged:	J.S. Bach, *Presto* from Violin Sonata in G, two versions; and:	
	Chaconne (Violin Partita in D minor), for piano left hand (1878)]	
Op.76	Eight Pieces, for piano (1879)	
Op.77	Violin Concerto in D (1879)	
Op.78	Violin Sonata No.1, in G (1879)	
[Edited:	Chopin, *Fantasia*, Op.49, *Barcarolle*, Op.60 (1879)]	

THE 1880s

Op.79	Two Rhapsodies, for piano (1880)	
~	Two Sets of Hungarian Dances, for piano duet (1880)	
[Edited:	Chopin, Sonata No.1, Op.4; *Mazurkas* (1880)]	
[Arranged:	Handel, six Continuo Realizations.(1880)]	
Op.80	'Academic Festival' Overture, for orchestra (1880, 1881)	
	(also arranged for piano duet)	
Op.81	'Tragic' Overture, for orchestra (1881)	
	(also arranged for piano duet)	
Op.82	*Nänie* (text by Schiller), for chorus & orchestra (1881)	
	(also arranged as piano score with text)	
Op.83	Piano Concerto No.2, in B flat (1882)	
	(also arranged for piano duet; and for two pianos)	
Op.84	Five Songs and Romances, for one or two voices (1882)	
Op.85	Six Songs (1882)	
Op.86	Six Songs (1882)	
Op.87	Piano Trio No.2, in C (1880/82, 1883)	

Op.88	String Quintet No.1, in F (1882) (also arranged for piano duet)
Op.89	*Gesang der Parzen* (Song of the Fates) (text by Goethe), for chorus & orchestra (1883)
Op.90	Symphony No.3, in F (1884) (also arranged for piano duet)
Op.91	Two Songs, for contralto, viola and piano (1884)
Op.92	Four Vocal Quartets, with piano (1874/84, 1884)
Op.93a	Six Songs & Romances for mixed chorus (1884)
Op.94	Five Songs (1884)
Op.95	Seven Songs (1884)
[Edited:	Schubert, Symphonies Nos.1–4 (1884) & 5–9 (1885)]
Op.93b	*Tafellied*, drinking song for six-part chorus & piano (1885)
~	Canon on a text by Uhland, for soprano & alto (1885)
Op.96	Four Songs (1886)
Op.97	Six Songs (1886)
Op.98	Symphony No.4, in E minor (1886) (also arranged for piano duet; and for two pianos)
Op.99	Cello Sonata No.2, in F (1887)
Op.100	Violin Sonata No.2, in A (1887)
Op.101	Piano Trio No.3, in C minor (1887)
Op.102	Double Concerto, for violin and cello, in A minor (1888)
Op.103	*Zigeunerlieder* (Gypsy Songs): Eleven, for vocal quartet with piano, and: Eight, from the above, arranged for voice & piano (1888)
Op.104	Five Partsongs, for mixed chorus (1888)
Op.105	Five Songs (1888)
Op.106	Five Songs (1888)
Op.107	Five Songs (1888)
Op.108	Violin Sonata No.3, in D minor (1886/88, 1889)

THE 1890s

Op.109	*Fest- und Gedenksprüche*, for chorus (1890) (also arranged as rehearsal piano score)

Op.110	Three Motets, for four- and eight-part mixed chorus (1890) (also arranged as rehearsal piano score)
Op.111	String Quintet No.2, in G (1890, 1891) (also arranged for piano duet)
Op.112	Six Vocal Quartets, with piano (1891)
Op.113	Thirteen Canons, for female voices
Op.8	Piano Trio No.1, in B, revised version (1891)
Op.114	Clarinet Trio, in A minor (1891, 1892) (option as piano trio)
Op.115	Clarinet Quintet, in G (1891, 1892)
Op.116	Seven Fantasias, for piano (1892)
Op.117	Three *Intermezzi*, for piano (1892)
Op.118	Six Pieces, for piano (1893)
Op.119	Four Pieces, for piano (1893)
~	Fifty-one Exercises, for piano (1893)
[Edited:	Schumann, nine posthumous works, various (1893)]
~	Forty-nine *Deutsche Volkslieder*, for voice & piano (various dates, 1894)
~	Thirty-two New Folksongs (various dates, 1926)
Op.120	Two Clarinet Sonatas (1894, 1895) (or for viola or violin): No.1, in F minor No.2, in E flat
Op.122	Eleven Chorale Preludes, for organ (various dates, 1902)
Op.121	*Vier ernste Gesänge* (Four Serious Songs) (1896)

SELECTED BIBLIOGRAPHY

The standard biography, which is still untranslated into English, is **Johannes Brahms** by Max Kalbeck (Berlin, 1904–14, reprinted 1974–75, in four volumes).

In German there are over twenty volumes of correspondence. The following translations are available:

Letters of Clara Schumann and Johannes Brahms (Vienna House, New York, 1973)

Johannes Brahms and Theodor Billroth: Letters from a Musical Friendship (University of Oklahoma Press, 1957)

The Herzogenberg Correspondence (London, 1909; Da Capo, New York, 1987)

Among other volumes of correspondence, Vienna House have issued one of **Letters to and from Joseph Joachim** that gives a fine flavour of his life as well as of | the times in which he and Brahms lived (New York, 1972).

Biographical studies of Brahms are numerous. The following is a good selection:

Recollections of Johannes Brahms by A. Dietrich & J.V. Widmann (London, 1904)

Life of Johannes Brahms by Florence May (Reeves, London, 1905, in two volumes)

Johannes Brahms, his Work and Personality by Hans Gal (Weidenfeld & Nicolson, London, 1963)

Johannes Brahms by Walter Niemann (London, 1929)

The Unknown Brahms by R.H. Schauffler (New York, 1933)

Johannes Brahms by Ivor Keys (Helm, London, 1989)

Among the most approachable studies of Brahms's music are the little **BBC Guides** (all published by BBC Publications):

Orchestral Music by John Horton
Chamber Music by Ivor Keys
Piano Music by Dennis Matthews
Songs by Eric Sams

For a more technical study of his music the following books can be recommended. Not all of Tovey's volumes contain essays on Brahms (but every volume is a delight whatever he writes on – and that includes Joachim's '*Hungarian*' *Violin Concerto*), whereas Musgrave does cover more or less all of the music.

Essays in Musical Analysis by Donald Francis Tovey (Oxford University Press, 1935–39, in seven volumes)

The Music of Brahms by Michael Musgrave (Oxford University Press, 1994)

Schoenberg's essay on Brahms as 'revolutionary' is to be found in **Style and Idea** by Arnold Schoenberg (Faber & Faber, London, 1975).

Index

THE
CLASSIC *f*M
GUIDE TO
CLASSICAL MUSIC

JEREMY NICHOLAS

'... *a fascinating and accessible guide ... it will provide*
an informative and illuminating source of insight
for everybody from the beginner to the musicologist.'

Sir Edward Heath

The Classic *f*M Guide to Classical Music opens with a masterly
history of classical music, illustrated with charts and lifelines, and
is followed by a comprehensive guide to more than 500 composers. There are major entries detailing the lives and works of the
world's most celebrated composers, as well as concise biographies
of more than 300 others.

This invaluable companion to classical music combines extensive
factual detail with fascinating anecdotes, and an insight into the
historical and musical influences of the great composers. It also
contains reviews and recommendations of the best works, and
extensive cross-references to lesser-known composers. Jeremy
Nicholas's vibrant, informative and carefully researched text is
complemented by photographs and cartoons, and is designed for
easy reference, with a comprehensive index.

£19.99   ISBN: 1 85793 760 0   **Hardback**
£9.99   ISBN: 1 86205 051 1   **Paperback**

CLASSIC *f*M
COMPACT COMPANIONS

CHOPIN, PUCCINI, ROSSINI, TCHAIKOVSKY

In association with *Classic fM* and *Philips Classics*, this revolutionary new series, *Compact Companions*, is a stylish package of book and compact disc. Each title provides the ultimate prelude to the lives and works of the most popular composers of classical music.

These composers' extraordinary, eventful lives and their power-ful, moving music make them the ideal subjects for combined reading and listening. Written by respected authors, the texts provide a comprehensive introduction to the life and work of the composer, and each includes a richly illustrated biography, a complete list of works and a definitive list of recommended recordings. The accompanying CD combines both favourite and less-well-known pieces, recorded by artists of world renown.

Chopin
Christopher Headington
ISBN: 1 85793 655 8

Puccini
Jonathon Brown
ISBN: 1 85793 660 4

Rossini
David Mountfield
ISBN: 1 85793 665 5

Tchaikovsky
David Nice
ISBN: 1 85793 670 1

£9.99 (inc. VAT) each companion

These books can be ordered direct from the publisher.
Please contact the Marketing Department.
But try your bookshop first.

CLASSIC *f*M LIFELINES

With 4.8 million listeners every week, *Classic fM* is now the most listened-to national commercial radio station in the UK. With the launch of *Classic fM Lifelines*, Pavilion Books and *Classic fM* are creating an affordable series of elegantly designed short biographies that will put everyone's favourite composers into focus.

Written with enthusiasm and in a highly accessible style, the *Classic fM Lifelines* series will become the Everyman of musical biographies. Titles for the series have been chosen from *Classic fM*'s own listener surveys of the most popular composers.

TITLES PUBLISHED:

Johannes Brahms
Jonathon Brown
ISBN: 1 85793 967 0

Claude Debussy
Jonathon Brown
ISBN: 1 85793 972 7

Edward Elgar
David Nice
ISBN: 1 85793 977 8

Gustav Mahler
Julian Haylock
ISBN: 1 85793 982 4

Sergei Rachmaninov
Julian Haylock
ISBN: 1 85793 944 1

Franz Schubert
Stephen Jackson
ISBN: 1 85793 987 5

£4.99 each book

FORTHCOMING TITLES:

- J.S. Bach
- Ludwig van Beethoven
- Benjamin Britten
- Joseph Haydn
- Dmitri Shostakovich
- Ralph Vaughan Williams

CLASSIC *f*M
LIFELINES

To purchase any of the books in the *Classic fM Lifelines* series
simply fill in the order form below and post or fax it,
together with your remittance, to the address below.

Please send the titles ticked below
(*published spring 1997)

Johannes Brahms ☐	*J.S. Bach	☐
Claude Debussy ☐	*Ludwig van Beethoven	☐
Edward Elgar ☐	*Benjamin Britten	☐
Gustav Mahler ☐	*Joseph Haydn	☐
Sergei Rachmaninov ☐	*Dmitri Shostakovich	☐
Franz Schubert ☐	*Ralph Vaughan Williams	☐

Number of titles @ £4.99 _____   Value: £_____
Add 10% of total value for postage and packing   Value: £_____
Total value of order: £_____

I enclose a cheque (UK only) payable to Pavilion Books Ltd ☐
OR
Please charge my credit card account ☐
I wish to pay by: Visa ☐ MasterCard ☐ Access ☐ American Express ☐

Card number ⬚⬚⬚⬚⬚⬚⬚⬚⬚⬚⬚⬚⬚⬚⬚⬚

Signature_____   Expiry Date_____
Name _____
Address_____
_____
_____   Postcode_____

Please send your order to: Marketing Department, Pavilion Books Ltd,
26 Upper Ground, London SE1 9PD, or fax for quick dispatch to:
Marketing Department, 0171-620 0042.